THE BRITISH FILM

The celebrated film director François Truffaut once famously observed that there was a certain incompatibility between the terms British and cinema. That was typical of the critical disparagement for so long suffered by British films. As late as 1969 a respected film scholar could dub British cinema 'the unknown cinema'. This was the situation because up to that time the critics, scholars and intellectuals writing about cinema preferred either continental films or latterly Hollywood to the homegrown product. Over the past thirty years that position has changed dramatically. There are now monographs, journals, book series, university courses and conferences entirely devoted to British cinema.

The Tauris British Film Guide series seeks to add to that process of revaluation by assessing in depth key British films from the past hundred years. Each film guide will establish the historical and cinematic context of the film, provide a detailed critical reading and assess the reception and after-life of the production. The series will draw on all genres and all eras and will over time build into a wide-ranging library of informed, in-depth books on the films that have defined British cinema. It is a publishing project that will comprehensively refute Truffaut's ill-informed judgement and demonstrate the variety, creativity, humanity, poetry and mythic power of the best of British cinema.

JEFFREY RICHARDS
General Editor, the British Film Guides

British Film Guides published and forthcoming:

The Charge of the Light Brigade Mark Connelly
The Dam Busters John Ramsden
Dracula Peter Hutchings
My Beautiful Laundrette Christine Geraghty
A Night to Remember Jeffrey Richards
The Private Life of Henry VIII Greg Walker
The Red Shoes Mark Connelly
The 39 Steps Mark Glancy
Whisky Galore! and The Maggie Colin McArthur

A BRITISH FILM GUIDE

A Night to Remember:
The Definitive *Titanic* Film

JEFFREY RICHARDS

I.B. TAURIS

LONDON · NEW YORK

Published in 2003 by I.B.Tauris & Co Ltd
6 Salem Road, London W2 4BU
175 Fifth Avenue, New York NY 10010
www.ibtauris.com

In the United States of America and Canada distributed by Palgrave
Macmillan a division of St Martin's Press, 175 Fifth Avenue, New York
NY 10010

ISBN 1 86064 849 5

A full CIP record for this book is available from the British Library
A full CIP record for this book is available from the Library of Congress

Library of Congress catalog card: available

Set in Monotype Fournier and Univers Black by Ewan Smith, London
Printed and bound in Great Britain by MPG Books, Bodmin

Contents

Illustrations / vi
Acknowledgements / viii

Film Credits   1
1 The Background   4
2 The Making of the Film   28
3 A Critical Analysis of the Film   59
4 Post-Production   85
5 The *Titanic* and the Cinema:
   After *A Night to Remember*   103

   Appendix: Nearer, My God, to Thee   116

   Notes   122
   Sources   128

Illustrations

1. Producer William MacQuitty and director Roy Baker inspect the scale model of the *Titanic*.   30

2. Great pains were taken to cast actors who resembled the historical originals: Captain E. J. Smith (left) and Laurence Naismith as Smith (right).   34

3. The upper class: the captain's table.   70

4. The lower class: the emigrants in steerage.   70

5. The middle class: the honeymooning Clarkes (Ronald Allen and Jill Dixon).   71

6. Mr and Mrs Isidor Straus (Meier Tzelniker and Helen Misener).   78

7. Romance blossoms between emigrants below deck.   78

8. Robert Lucas (John Merivale), devoted husband and father, persuades his wife (Honor Blackman) and children to leave the ship by pretending that there is nothing serious happening.   79

9. Wireless operator John Phillips (Kenneth Griffith) stays at his post until the end.   82

10. Chairman Bruce Ismay (Frank Lawton) saves his life by escaping in a lifeboat with the women and children.   82

11. Professional gamblers Hoyle (Redmond Phillips) and Yates (Ralph Michael) meet different ends: Hoyle escapes in a half-filled lifeboat, Yates swims away from an upturned boat so as not to overload it.   83

12. Robert Lucas (John Merivale) hands over his sleeping son to Second Officer Lightoller (Kenneth More) and remains on board to go down with the ship.   83

13. Although the film prided itself on its factual accuracy, this launching ceremony never in fact took place. Designer Thomas Andrews (Michael Goodliffe) and Chairman Bruce Ismay (Frank Lawton) flank the unnamed lady.   88

14. Spectacular re-creation of the flooding of the engine rooms.   88

15. Whether or not the steerage passengers were locked below decks and, if so, why is still hotly disputed.   89

16. Kenneth More as Lightoller evacuating passengers. His character
    was given several actions performed by other officers on the night.   89

17. Kenneth More as Lightoller attempts to prevent panicking passengers
    swamping the lifeboats.   92

18. Captain Rostron (Anthony Bushell) orders the *Carpathia* to steam to
    the aid of the *Titanic*.   92

19. The ship's orchestra play music to calm the passengers.   93

20. The *Titanic* sinks.   93

21. Second Officer Lightoller (Kenneth More) and Colonel Gracie
    (James Dyrenforth) try to make sense of the tragedy.   95

Acknowledgements

A great many friends and colleagues have provided advice and assistance of various kinds and I acknowledge my grateful thanks to them for all they have done to speed the production of this monograph: Dr Anthony Aldgate, Mr Michael Coyne, Dr Nigel Dalziel, Dr Alan Finlayson, Dr Mark Glancy, Ms Thelma Goodman, Dr Kevin Gough-Yates, Mr Bernard Hrusa Marlow, Mr Andrew Ison, Professor John M. MacKenzie, Professor Brian McFarlane, Professor Vincent Porter, Ms Pat Robinson, Dr Andrew Spicer and Professor Richard Taylor. I am grateful to Mr Jeffrey Hulbert for valuable research assistance, and to the staffs of Lancaster University Library, the British Film Institute, and the National Film Archive for their help.

My greatest debt is to Roy Ward Baker and William MacQuitty, not only because they made the film but because they generously granted me lengthy interviews to supplement what I had already learned from their autobiographies, Roy Ward Baker's *The Director's Cut* and William MacQuitty's *A Life to Remember*, and from William MacQuitty's *Titanic Memories* and the documentary film *The Making of A Night to Remember* (1993), to which Mr MacQuitty contributed an extensive interview and his fascinating behind-the-scenes home movie footage of the shooting of the film. I respectfully dedicate this book to them.

Stills were provided by the British Film Institute (Stills Department) and are used by courtesy of Carlton International Media Ltd. They are reproduced here for the purposes of critical analysis.

For Roy Ward Baker and
William MacQuitty

Film Credits

A NIGHT TO REMEMBER

Production Company	Rank Organisation
Distributors	Rank Film Distributors
Director	Roy Baker
Producer	William MacQuitty
Screenplay	Eric Ambler (based on the book by Walter Lord)
Music	William Alwyn (played by the Sinfonia of London, conducted by Muir Mathieson)
Director of Photography	Geoffrey Unsworth
Art Director	Alex Vetchinsky
Editor	Sidney Hayers
Special Effects	Bill Warrington
Special Effects Photography	Skeets Kelly
Production Controller	Arthur Alcott
Production Manager	Jack Hanbury
Assistant Director	Robert Asher
Camera Operator	David Harcourt
Continuity	Penny Daniels
Costume Designer	Yvonne Caffin
Makeup	W. F. Partleton
Hairdresser	Pauline Trent
Sound Editor	Harry Miller
Sound Recordists	Geoffrey Daniels, Gordon K. McCallum
Set Dresser	Len Townsend
Executive Producer	Earl St John
Length	11,063 feet
Running Time	123 minutes
UK Première	3 July 1958
US Première	16 December 1958

CAST

Kenneth More	Second Officer Charles Herbert Lightoller
Ronald Allen	Mr Clarke

Robert Ayres	Major Arthur Peuchen
Honor Blackman	Mrs Lucas
Anthony Bushell	Captain Arthur Rostron
John Cairney	Murphy
Jill Dixon	Mrs Clarke
Jane Downs	Mrs Sylvia Lightoller
James Dyrenforth	Colonel Archibald Gracie
Michael Goodliffe	Thomas Andrews
Kenneth Griffith	John Phillips
Harriette Johns	Lady Richard
Frank Lawton	The Chairman (J. Bruce Ismay)
Richard Leech	First Officer William Murdoch
David McCallum	Harold Bride
Alec McCowen	Harold Cottam
Tucker McGuire	Molly Brown
John Merivale	Robert Lucas
Ralph Michael	Jay Yates
Laurence Naismith	Captain E. J. Smith
Russell Napier	Captain Stanley Lord
Redmond Phillips	Hoyle
George Rose	Baker Charles Joughin
Joseph Tomelty	Dr William O'Loughlin
Patrick Waddington	Sir Richard
Jack Watling	Fourth Officer Joseph Boxhall
Geoffrey Bayldon	Harold Evans
Michael Bryant	Sixth Officer James Moody
Cyril Chamberlain	Quartermaster George Rowe
Richard Clarke	Martin Gallagher
Bee Duffell	Mrs Farrell
Harold Goldblatt	Benjamin Guggenheim
Gerald Harper	Third Officer, *Carpathia*
Richard Hayward	Victualling Manager
Thomas Heathcote	Third Steward
Danuta Karell	Polish Mother
Andrew Keir	Second Engineer James Hesketh
Christina Lubicz	Polish Girl
Patrick McAlinney	James Farrell
Barry McGregor	Apprentice James Gibson, *Californian*
Eddie Malin	Fifth Steward
Helen Misener	Mrs Ida Straus
Mary Monaghan	Kate
Howard Pays	Fifth Officer Harold Lowe
Philip Ray	Reverend Anderson
Harold Siddons	Second Officer Herbert Stone , *Californian*
Julian Somers	Mr Bull

Theresa Thorne	Edith Russell
Tim Turner	Third Officer Charles Groves, *Californian*
Meier Tzelniker	Isidor Straus

(uncredited)

Roger Avon	Look-out Reginald Lee
Charles Belchier	Orchestra Leader
Olwen Brookes	Miss Evans
Henry Campbell	W. T. Stead
Pauline Challoner	Lucas Child
Donald Churchill	Passenger
George A. Cooper	Purser, *Carpathia*
Grace Denbigh-Russell	Woman
John Dunbar	Scotsman
Gay Emma	Lucas Child
Bernard Fox	Look-out Frederick Fleet
Jonathan Hanson	Hysterical Man
Paul Hardwick	Guggenheim's Valet
Gladys Henson	Hysterical Woman
Glyn Houston	Stoker
Robert James	Engineer
Stratford Johns	Crewman
Ann Lancaster	Mrs Bull
Howard Lang	Chief Officer Henry Wilde
Desmond Llewellyn	Steward
Stephen Lowe	Tom Lucas
Derren Nesbitt	Third Stoker
Etain O'Dell	Irish Girl
Maureen O'Reilly	Irish Girl
Hal Osmond	Steward no. 20
Steve Plytas	Argumentative Foreigner
Robert Raglan	Chief Engineer, *Carpathia*
George Roderick	Steward
Norman Rossington	Steward no. 14
Robert Scroggins	Ship's Boy
Richard Shaw	Crewman
Charles Stapley	Passenger
Marianne Stone	Stewardess no. 2
Jack Stuart	Stoker
Alma Taylor	Old Lady
John Warren	Crewman
Russell Waters	Chief Clerk, Victualling Department
Gordon Whiting	Clerk, Victualling Department

ONE
■■■■ The Background ■■■■

On the night of 14/15 April 1912, the White Star Company's liner *RMS Titanic*, the largest and most luxurious ship in the world, on its maiden voyage from Southampton to New York, struck an iceberg and sank. There were 2,201 people on board and the lifeboats had capacity only for 1,178. The Captain, Edward John Smith, ordered the lifeboats filled with the women and children first and in the event some lifeboats left half-empty. Of the 2,201 people on board *Titanic*, 1,490 died and 711 survived.[1]

The iceberg was struck at 11.40 p.m. and the ship went down at 2.20 a.m. Just after 4.00 a.m. the Cunard liner *Carpathia*, commanded by Captain Arthur Rostron, which, alerted by an SOS signal from *Titanic*, had raced to the scene, arrived to pick up survivors. Captain Smith perished along with the ship's designer Thomas Andrews and the large majority of the crew (all the engineers, all the pursers, all the ship's boys, all the musicians). Only 23 per cent of the crew were saved. It was the greatest maritime disaster in history and it sent a thrill of horror round the world. The ship had been pronounced 'practically unsinkable'; yet a score of celebrities, the rich, the famous and the distinguished, perished in the icy seas. Among them were American millionaires John Jacob Astor, Benjamin Guggenheim, Charles Hays, George Widener, John B. Thayer and Isidor Straus with his wife Ida; Major Archibald Butt, an aide to President Taft; the detective story writer Jacques Futrelle, the 'American Conan Doyle'; the painter Francis Millet; the theatrical producer Henry B. Harris and the journalist W. T. Stead.

Two formal investigations by the US Congress and the British Board of Trade were held. The congressional investigation, headed by Republican Senator William Smith Alden, criticized the 'absolute unpreparedness' of the crew to deal with an emergency; the lax regulations of the British Board of Trade which prescribed too few lifeboats; and the 'over-confidence' of Captain Smith. The British inquiry was headed by a former judge, Lord Mersey, and, although some have suggested it was a whitewash, his report is described by the British historian Richard Howells as 'the most sober and detailed documentary account available' and by American writer Stephen Cox as 'a monument of intelligent and well-grounded diversity of judgement'.[2] Mersey found that the entire passage had been made at high speed but not maximum speed and that the Captain had not been ordered by the owners to break the transatlantic record as was being alleged. He acquitted Captain Smith of negligence. He regretted that there had been no proper boat drill (because the law did not require it) and that some of the half-empty lifeboats had not sought to save the passengers in the water. He regretted that the Leyland liner *Californian*, under Captain Lord, stopped by ice between five and ten miles away, had failed to respond to the distress rockets. Had it done so, it might have saved lives. The Board of Trade required sixteen lifeboats for all vessels over 10,000 tons and the *Titanic* had twenty but still not enough for the number of passengers. The inquiry recommended that in future there should be sufficient lifeboats for all those on board all ships, watertight bulkheads, a twenty-four-hour wireless service on all ships, regular boat, fire and watertight door drills, and the reduction of speed on the receipt of ice warnings.

From the moment news of the sinking broke, the story of the *Titanic* became encrusted with myth.[3] The *Titanic* went down at a time of acute tension and disturbance in both Britain and America. In the United States, the Republican Party had split between the adherents of William Howard Taft and those of Theodore Roosevelt. Race relations were embittered (sixty-one blacks were lynched in 1912), labour relations had become violent with the Industrial Workers of the World (the Wobblies) fighting against the police and vigilantes in defence of labour rights and free speech, and there was a heated debate around moves to restrict immigration to the United States. The agitation for women's suffrage was increasing and the largest suffragette demonstration in history occurred at the same time as the funeral of *Titanic* victim John Jacob Astor on 4 May. In Britain, suffragette agitation had turned violent (in 1913 Emily Davidson threw herself under the King's horse at the Derby) and there was continuing labour unrest. A ten-month miners' strike in Wales (1910–11) had been followed in 1912 by a national railway strike. Politics was inflamed by the crisis over Irish Home Rule. Unrest in the Balkans and the continuing naval and military build-up by Germany were paving the way for the outbreak of war in 1914.

The *Titanic* story provided the opportunity to underline and affirm the basic values of a culture and a social structure that were under threat. Each of the key stories associated with the disaster provided evidence of real-life conduct based on enduring values and served to refute the ideas of socialism, feminism and anti-capitalism that were challenging the status quo.

The order of evacuation ('women and children first') confirmed the idea of women as helpless creatures who needed protection and cast the men as those protectors, stoic, self-sacrificing and noble. The much-repeated story of Mrs Ida Straus insisting on remaining with her husband of forty years, Isidor Straus, and perishing with him endorsed the sanctity of marriage and served to refute those who attacked it as patriarchal tyranny.

When Benjamin Guggenheim and his valet appeared without their lifebelts, saying, 'We've dressed up in our best and are prepared to go down like gentlemen', they were endorsing the code of chivalry that was shared by the cultures of Britain and America.[4] The idea of the gentleman and the code associated with it had been the dominant model of mascu-linity in both countries for a century or more. Gentlemanliness was not, as Richard Howells has suggested, associated specifically with social class.[5] It transcended class. As Victorian guru Samuel Smiles put it: 'Riches and rank have no necessary connexion with genuine gentlemanly qualities. The poor man may be a true gentleman – in spirit and daily life. He may be honest, truthful, upright, polite, temperate, courageous, self-respecting and self-helping – that is, be a true gentleman.'[6]

This is why the British Admiral Lord Charles Beresford could des-cribe Captain Smith of the *Titanic*, by origin working-class, as 'an example of the very best type of British seaman and British gentleman' and say that the behaviour of everyone on board had been 'chivalrous', and the American Champ Clark, Speaker of the House, could praise the 'chivalric behaviour of the men on the ill-fated ship'.[7] The behaviour of the men of whatever social class and whether British or American on the *Titanic* endorsed chivalry as the dominant mode of masculinity.

Captain Smith's reported injunction to his crew 'Be British', which was engraved on his memorial statue in Lichfield, endorsed the idea of Britishness being equated with the 'stiff upper lip', shorthand for stoicism, emotional restraint, sense of duty, self-discipline and lack of hysteria. In Britain, this distinctive character was seen as justification for the suprem-acy of the British Empire. It was reported of Captain Smith that 'he believed with all his heart and soul in the British Empire'.[8] Second Officer

Lightoller wrote later: 'Never in my life have I been so unspeakably proud of the English-speaking race as I was during that night. The cool, calm, unselfish courage exemplified throughout has never been excelled.'[9] It was no coincidence that the *Titanic* memorial concert was held on Empire Day. This stoical concept of Britishness applied in a wider sense to the whole Anglo-Saxon race and thus included the Americans, permitting American survivor Colonel Archibald Gracie to observe: 'The coolness, courage and sense of duty that I here witnessed made me thankful to God and proud of my Anglo-Saxon race that gave this perfect and superb exhibition of self-control at this hour of severest trial.'[10] The *Atlanta Constitution* thought that the exemplary conduct of the Anglo-Saxons justified white supremacy in the world: 'The Anglo-Saxon may yet boast that his sons are fit to rule the earth so long as men choose death with the courage they must have displayed when the great liner crashed into the mountains of ice, and the aftermath brought its final test.'[11]

By contrast, where there was panic it was by 'Latins'. Fifth Officer Harold Lowe reported having to hold back 'Italians and Latins' by gunfire – shots fired into the air – to prevent them storming the boats. The Italian Ambassador to the United States protested and the word Italian was withdrawn. But popular belief was confirmed in the essential superiority of the Anglo-Saxon over the Latin races. Guggenheim and the Strauses were Jewish but by their conduct they became honorary Anglo-Saxons.

Finally, the story that the ship's band was playing the hymn 'Nearer, My God, to Thee', as the ship went down confirmed the Christian stoicism and resignation of the victims and the continuing validity of Christianity in the face of the rise of Darwinism, Freudianism, Marxism and the other intellectual challenges to the faith.

These stories and incidents instantly promoted in newspaper reports and thereafter perpetuated in books, songs, postcards, statues and memorials, became indelible parts of the *Titanic* myth, so widely known and so regularly recycled that any film version would need to take account of them.

Along with the positive and uplifting elements of the myth, there were some darker views of the tragedy. First there is the idea of class discrimination in the matter of survival. The class basis of the survivors, which indicated a strict social hierarchy even in death, was to become a cause of indictment in changed times. The idea of 'women and children first' is not a fiction. Far more women than men survived: 94 per cent of first-class women, 81 per cent of second-class women and 47 per cent of steerage women, compared to 31 per cent of first-class men, 10 per cent of second-class and 14 per cent of steerage-class men. But overall, 60 per cent of first-class passengers survived, 44 per cent second-class and only 25 per cent of steerage-class.[12] Little attention was paid to steerage-class passengers in contemporary reports and inquiries. The *New York Times* (20 April 1912) reported: 'All disorderly conduct, and there was enough to cause bloodshed, occurred among the steerage passengers.' A survivor from New York reported: 'everybody in the first and second cabins behaved splendidly. The members of the crew behaved magnificently. But some men in third-class, presumably passengers, were shot by officers. Who these men were we do not know.'[13]

There were rumours that third-class passengers had been deliberately locked below decks. One migrant reported a gate being locked and broken down by steerage passengers. But Michael Davie concludes that there is 'no evidence that it was general ship's policy to keep the steerage passengers back while the rest escaped'.[14] The Mersey Inquiry examined the charge that the third-class passengers had been prevented from reaching the boat deck and the first- and second-class had been given precedence in entering the boats. Mersey concluded:

> There appears to have been no truth in these suggestions. It is no doubt true that the proportion of third class passengers saved falls far short of the proportion of the first and second class, but this is accounted for by the greater reluctance of the third-class passengers to leave the ship, by the difficulty in getting them up from their quarters, which were at the extreme ends of the ship, by their unwillingness to part with their baggage, and by other similar causes … I am satisfied … that the third-class passengers were not unfairly treated.[15]

The fact that many of the emigrants – they included Italians, Syrians, Armenians, Russians, Chinese, Scandinavians, Dutch and Irish – could not speak English added to their predicament. This is confirmed by Mersey's finding that 'of the Irish emigrants in the third class', who could of course speak English, 'a large proportion was saved'.[16] Richard Howells, endorsing this, wryly observes: 'if any of the doors between third-class and other areas of the ship had been locked, this was not in anticipation of shipwreck, but in compliance with US immigration laws. These made segregation mandatory on immigrant ships in the interests of immigration control and the feared spread of infectious diseases.'[17]

Second, there is the idea of the judgement of God. It was reported that a deck hand had said to Mrs Albert Caldwell, 'God himself could not sink this ship'.[18] Some Christian ministers in both Britain and America saw the *Titanic* both as an embodiment of the false values of the modern age – the 'floating palace' of conspicuous consumption, luxury, greed and pride – struck down by God's wrath, and as an example of the technological *hubris* ('the unsinkable ship') of a godless modern age being followed by divinely inspired *nemesis*. In England the Bishop of Winchester, preaching at the memorial service for Captain Smith, said the disaster was a mighty lesson against our security and confidence and trust in the strength of machinery and money: 'The name *Titanic* will stand as a monument of warning against human presumption.'[19]

The First World War overtook the tragedy of the *Titanic* and in retrospect it came to be seen as a precursor of the destruction of the Edwardian world that the war precipitated. There was not to be such a flurry of interest in the subject as occurred in 1912 and 1913 until the 1950s. In 1953, 20th Century-Fox produced a major film, *Titanic*, and this was followed by the publication of Walter Lord's book *A Night to Remember* in 1955, which was on the bestseller list for six months. This meticulous documentary account was published in Britain in 1956, came out in paperback the same year and has never been out of print since. A live television adaptation of the book was produced on NBC in 1956 and the British film version *A Night to Remember* was released by Rank in 1958. In 1960 there was a Broadway musical, *The Unsinkable Molly Brown*, about one of the American heroines of the disaster.

The next upsurge of interest came in the 1980s and 1990s and still continues. Lord Grade's thriller *Raise the Titanic!*, about a successful bid to recover the wreck, was a legendary box-office disaster in 1980. But in 1985 the wreck of the *Titanic* was located by a Franco-American expedition led by Dr Robert Ballard. The wreck was filmed and artefacts retrieved. This stirred the imagination of the world. Walter Lord produced a sequel to his classic book, *The Night Lives On* (1986), in which in the light of thirty years' further research he meditated on such issues as the final music, the nature of the damage, the compensation claims, the role of the *Californian* and so forth. There was now a flood of books and television documentaries and then a television mini-series *Titanic* (1996), a full-scale Broadway musical *Titanic* (1997), and the James Cameron cinema blockbuster *Titanic* (1997). Sherlock Holmes turned up on the *Titanic* in William Seil's ingenious novel *Sherlock Holmes and the Titanic Tragedy* (1996).

What has been the continuing appeal of the myth? In the preface to the 1976 illustrated edition of his book, Walter Lord, doyen of *Titanic* scholars, wrote: 'To social historians it is a microcosm of the early 1900s. To nautical enthusiasts it is the ultimate shipwreck. To students of human nature it is an endlessly fascinating laboratory. For lovers of nostalgia it has the allure of yesterday. For day-dreamers, it has all those might-have-beens.' Lord also drew a moral:

> Overriding everything else, the *Titanic* marked the end of a general feeling of confidence. Until then men felt they had found the answer to a steady, orderly, civilized life. For 100 years the Western world had been at peace. For 100 years technology had steadily improved. For 100 years the benefits of peace and industry seemed to be filtering satisfactorily through society. In retrospect there may seem less grounds for confidence, but at the time most articulate people felt life was all right. The *Titanic* woke them up. Never again would they be quite sure of themselves.[20]

This a very partial and retrospective view. There had not been peace for one hundred years before the *Titanic*. That century had seen the 1848 revolutions, the American Civil War, the Franco-Prussian War, the Boer War and countless colonial conflicts. At the time the *Titanic* went down, both British and American societies were convulsed with disorders of various kinds. But from the perspective of 1955, in the aftermath of two world wars, the Holocaust and the atomic bomb, the Edwardian era had assumed the golden haze of an idyll and the *Titanic* came to seem the harbinger of the terrible events of the twentieth century.

For other writers the year 1912, which saw not only the wreck of the *Titanic* but the deaths of Captain Scott and his companions after they failed to reach the South Pole first, became a potent symbol of challenge to the prevailing social system. This is why Terence Rattigan set his 1946 play *The Winslow Boy* in 1912 and why J. B. Priestley set his plays *Eden End* (1934) and *An Inspector Calls* (1948) in 1912. But each generation has rewritten the myth of the *Titanic* to fit its own prejudices and preoccupations, and ideas of gender, class and nation have been inscribed in each recycling of the story. The cinema has played a major role in the evolving myth of the *Titanic*.

THE *TITANIC* AND THE CINEMA: *BEFORE A NIGHT TO REMEMBER*

Within days of the disaster the newsreel companies in Britain and America were running items on the *Titanic*. But there was no film of the maiden voyage of the liner and there seem to have been only some half a dozen sequences of the *Titanic* ever shot. They include scenes of the ship in Belfast and scenes at Southampton prior to the maiden voyage. The companies mostly had to make do with scenes of the *Titanic*'s sister ship *Olympic*, footage of Captain Smith aboard the *Olympic*, shots of the putative site of the sinking and sequences involving the survivors arriving in New York and the memorial service at St Paul's Cathedral in London. 'Nearer, My God, to Thee' was often played to accompany the newsreels.

One of the many remarkable features of the story of the *Titanic* was the presence on board of film actress Dorothy Gibson returning with her mother from a vacation in Europe. She and her mother survived and, once safely back in New York, she immediately appeared in a film reconstruction of the disaster, *Saved from the Titanic*, for Eclair Films. Shot aboard a derelict transport vessel in New York harbour and featuring Dorothy in the actual dress she wore on the night of the sinking, it was being shown in cinemas a month after the event. *Moving Picture World* (10 May 1912) described it as 'a heart-stirring tale of the sea's greatest tragedy depicted by an eye witness'.

A German film version of the tragedy, *Night and Ice (Titanic: In Nacht und Eis)*, running about forty minutes, was shot in 1912, partly at Cuxhaven and Hamburg utilizing a real liner and partly in the Continental Film Studios, Berlin. Directed by Mime Misu, it contained ten main scenes: the departure of the *Titanic*, life aboard, on the open sea, *soirée dansante*, the iceberg, the collision, the launching of the lifeboats, courage and sacrifice, 'Nearer, My God, to Thee', and the wrecking of the ship. As with the newsreels, some showings of the film were accompanied by the music of 'Nearer, My God, to Thee'. The film was released in Germany, France, Scandinavia, the Netherlands and the United States.[21]

The first talkie to re-create the *Titanic* tragedy was *Atlantic* (1929), based on the play by Ernest Raymond. Ernest Raymond had achieved notable success with his novel *Tell England* (1922) about the military disaster of Gallipoli where he served as an army chaplain. He hit upon another disaster as the subject for a play, *The Berg*, which would cover the final two hours of the *Titanic*'s life from the moment the iceberg is first glimpsed through to the last minutes before the ship goes down. It is probably no coincidence that Raymond's play appeared in 1929. It was only three years since the General Strike had paralysed the country and awakened very real fears of revolution. It also came at the end of a decade which had seen the 'bright young things' challenging conventional morality, the 'flappers' overturning established ideas of femininity, and a record divorce rate. Many commentators feared social and moral collapse. It was the appropriate context in which to remind the public of the values embodied in the *Titanic* myth.

Raymond created a mixed group of characters and charted their reactions to the crisis. But the central theme is the clash of world-views between a crippled atheist novelist John Rool and an Anglican padre who is losing faith in his vocation. Rool resolves to help the passengers meet a noble end, but the padre comes into his own at the end with Christian consolation.

Jack De Leon, who ran the small suburban Q Theatre, Kew, thought the play 'devastatingly tragic and superbly written' and put it on with a fine cast headed by Godfrey Tearle as Rool and George Relph as the padre.[22] It opened on 4 March 1929. *The Times* (5 March 1929) called it a 'study in fortitude' and noted that when the crisis came, 'they all behave with the same quiet heroism'. The play was deemed rather contrived and schematic and the last act 'distinctly inferior' but the reviewer concluded that 'it was well acted throughout and made a good impression'. It transferred with the same cast to His Majesty's Theatre in the West End on 12 March where it ran for less than a month, though it later became a standard item with repertory theatres and amateur dramatic companies. However, before the end of the West End run, British International Pictures had purchased the film rights. They immediately initiated an epic film version, *Atlantic*, shot simultaneously in English-, French- and German-language versions with three different casts by German director E. A. Dupont. This was briefly standard practice before the perfection of dubbing. The film script by Victor Kendall largely dropped the intellectual conflict between Rool and the padre, eliminated the padre's crisis of faith, and, recalled Raymond, 'went, full sail, for the external drama only, which was almost fool-proof and actor-proof'.[23]

The adaptation introduced a whole range of details that made it clear that the inspiration was the *Titanic* disaster. The flat calm and clear sky are commented on. There is discussion of the danger of ice-floes and the fact that the ship is unsinkable. The ship hits an iceberg and is holed below the waterline. The engine room begins to flood and Captain Collins orders all passengers to don lifejackets and women and children to enter the lifeboats, claiming it is merely a drill. The watertight doors are closed and distress rockets are fired. As word of the ship's fate spreads, the passengers panic, some men rush the boats at one stage and

Please add my name to your mailing list to receive details of books in the following subject areas

Middle East ☐   Archaeology & Ancient History ☐   Asian Studies ☐

Islamic Studies ☐   Art & Architecture ☐   Central Asia ☐

Iran ☐   Film / Media / Visual Culture ☐   Human Geography ☐

Jewish Studies ☐   Politics, Intl. Relations & Defence ☐   Modern History ☐

Women's Studies ☐   Russia & Former Soviet Union ☐   African Studies ☐

My other areas of interest are:...

Name..

Address...

....

....

Postcode.. Email address.............................. Date...............

Your requests can also be directed to marketing@ibtauris.com

TAURIS
I.B. TAURIS PUBLISHERS

I.B. Tauris & Co Ltd
6 Salem Road
London
W2 4BU
United Kingdom

are shot by the officers. The captain releases the crew, saying, 'Men, you have done your duty. You can do no more now. It's every man for himself.' The wireless operator abandons his lifejacket and continues to send out an SOS. The band, on deck in their lifejackets, play dance music to calm the passengers, ending with 'Nearer, My God, to Thee', as the ship is about to go down.

The film was shot at the British International Studios at Elstree with exteriors filmed aboard a P & O liner at Tilbury Docks, probably the *Mooltan*.[24] When the White Star Line got wind of the project, they wrote to BIP to urge that the film be dropped because of the painful memories it would rouse and the adverse effect it would have on the shipping business, already hit by the depression. BIP answered them by saying there would be no reference to the *Titanic* – the ship had been renamed *Atlantic*. According to Simon Mills, certain scenes in the script were trimmed to reduce the most obvious echoes of the *Titanic* (such as Captain Collins's injunction to the crew 'Be British') but enough remained to leave audiences in no doubt about the film's inspiration.[25] *The Times* report (29 October 1929) of the German version's première was headed 'Film of the Titanic shown in Berlin'. The White Star Line complained bitterly to the Board of Trade but to no effect.

The German-language version of *Atlantic* opened in Berlin on 28 October 1929 and was the first German-language talkie to be seen in Germany. Its distinguished cast included Fritz Kortner, Willi Forst, Franz Lederer and Lucie Mannheim and *The Times* Berlin correspondent, describing the disaster scenes as 'very impressive', reported that the film was received with 'prolonged applause'. The reception for the British version, first shown on 17 November 1929, was more mixed.

The Times reflected the general critical opinion that the actual scenes of the disaster – the ship sinking, the lifeboats launched, the rising panic 'among all grades of the *Atlantic*'s cosmopolitan population' – were 'superb'. But the film was let down by its dialogue, which condemned 'a number of distinguished English actors' to deliver 'a number of highly undistinguished words'. Franklin Dyall did all he could 'to give an air of profundity to John Rool's sententiousness' but was ultimately defeated by his dialogue and Ellaline Terriss as his wife suffered in 'a ridiculously inadequate part'.[26]

The film pioneered the *Grand Hotel* format for the *Titanic* genre: the mixed group of passengers whose lives reach crisis point as the ship sinks. Much of the action of the film, like that of the play, takes place in the first-class bar of the *Atlantic*, where the major figures gather:

cynical crippled author John Rool; married philanderer Tate-Hughes who is conducting an illicit affair with a female passenger; newly-weds Laurence and Monica; pukka military figure Major Boldy; comical little Latin 'Dandy'; and the padre. When the ship strikes the iceberg, Lanchester, the Second Officer, privately tells Rool that the ship has only three hours to live, and Rool determines to ensure that the leading characters behave well, so he tells them privately about the fate of the ship. Tate-Hughes does everything he can to persuade his wife and daughter (who know about his adultery and are respectively hurt and disgusted) to get into the lifeboats. They refuse until Rool tells them the ship is doomed and he is trying to save their lives. They regain respect for him and follow his orders to enter the lifeboat while he remains behind. Laurence persuades the reluctant Monica to enter the lifeboat; but confides in Rool his distress that he must leave her as she is pregnant. This echoes the predicament of John Jacob and Madeleine Astor. When Laurence later faints from the tension, Rool (who was going to be put into a lifeboat as a cripple) gives up his place and orders Lanchester to put Laurence in the boat in his place, which he does. Rool's wife insists on staying with him, recalling the reaction of Mrs Ida Straus.

The aspects of the myth that are embodied here are that, for the most part, the leading characters behave well; Tate-Hughes redeemed from his adultery, Rool cured of his cynicism. It ends with the triumph of spirituality. When 'Nearer, My God, to Thee' is played, everyone joins in and the film like the play ends in the bar with the assembled characters calm and resigned led by the padre in the Lord's Prayer as the water floods in. The lights go on and off and are finally extinguished altogether and all we hear in the darkness is the screaming and the final plunge of the ship.

The only leading character to panic is the foreigner 'Dandy'. Lanchester, the epitome of the stiff-upper-lip Anglo-Saxon throughout, puts his hand on his arm and says 'Steady. See it through, old man', and Rool encourages him with the words of W. E. Henley's poem *Invictus*: 'I am the master of my fate – I am the captain of my soul.' When some men rush one of the boats, one of them is a black. There were historically no blacks on board *Titanic* among either passengers or crew, but, like 'Dandy's' panic, this serves to underline Anglo-Saxon stoicism by contrast with the conduct of 'inferior' races.

The leading characters are all middle-class, apart from Rool's valet Pointer who behaves as well as the rest, and, apart from 'Dandy', all are British. The only American is a gambler who appears in the final scenes and initiates a poker game. The only real reference to class comes at the end when the steward leads the crew into the bar saying, 'We're all one class now'; some get drunk, some play cards, some just wait, but all join in the prayer at the end. The Captain asks Lanchester to take a little girl who has been left behind and swim to one of the lifeboats. He obeys, takes the girl, dives in and swims off towards a boat. The film, then, specifically endorses the values highlighted in the Edwardian myth of the *Titanic*: Anglo-Saxon superiority, chivalry, stoicism, marriage and Christian spirituality, all of them still part of the dominant ideology in inter-war Britain, and all being re-emphasized at a time of profound social and cultural anxiety.

When Ernest Raymond saw the film, he pronounced it 'a pretentious and grandiose film with many fine spectacular scenes and some intolerably silly ones', which was very much the opinion of the British critics.[27] Seen today, that verdict still stands. The scenes of the abandonment of the ship, the surging mobs, the rising panic, have a graphic immediacy which shows up the sluggish pace and stagey tone of the rest of the film. Director E. A. Dupont is revealed as one of the most spectacular casualties of sound. He had achieved a considerable reputation as a director in Germany with his drama *Variety* (1925), a powerful drama of passion and jealousy set in a circus. He came to England to explore similar themes in two impressive films, *Piccadilly* (1928) and *Moulin Rouge* (1928), which confirmed his mastery of silent storytelling, conveying everything by movement, gesture and posture with the minimum use of inter-titles. But he proved incapable of handling English dialogue. He displayed in his early talkies *Atlantic* and *Cape Forlorn* a fondness for the pregnant pause which extended his films unconscionably and slowed them to a funereal pace. In *Atlantic*, this resulted in otherwise capable actors turning in extraordinarily stilted performances. John Longden as Lanchester was condemned to much lip-chewing and sonorously unreal delivery. Madeleine Carroll as Monica sounds as if she is acting in a foreign language, unable to place the correct emphases on words.

Director Victor Saville blamed Dupont's limited understanding of English which slowed down the English cast: 'the actors had to speak deliberately so that the director himself could understand the dialogue'.[28] Remnants of Dupont's previously fluid visual style remain in scenes without dialogue. But aside from the actual disaster scenes, Dupont is well and truly sunk by the weight of words. The German version, in which all the characters become Germans, is superior to the British, although the camera set-ups and scene stagings are identical.[29] It is better acted and the dialogue is naturalistic, conversational and largely devoid of pregnant pauses. Despite this, much of the production has the static nature of the filmed stage play which was the bane of the early talkies. Dupont was never to recover his directorial stature and ended up as a refugee director in Hollywood making undistinguished B pictures.

Although there was to be no full-length *Titanic* film made in Hollywood until 1953, the memory of the *Titanic* was kept before the public by periodic allusions in films. In 1932, the Fox Film Corporation filmed Noël Coward's stage play *Cavalcade*, which was to win Oscars for Best Picture and Best Director (Frank Lloyd). During the course of the film, Edward and Edith Marryot take their honeymoon trip on the *Titanic* and both are lost. The scene of the couple on the deck of the liner – with Coward's stage direction that 'Nearer, My God, to Thee' be played – was reproduced in the film.

In 1937 Walter Wanger produced and Frank Borzage directed the romantic melodrama *History is Made at Night* with Charles Boyer, Jean Arthur and Colin Clive. The action centred on a love triangle between a shipowner (Colin Clive), his wife Irene (Jean Arthur) and her French head-waiter lover, Paul (Charles Boyer). The pathologically jealous shipping magnate, who is called Bruce-Vail not Ismay-, frames his wife's lover for murder. Vail is American but played in pukka British style by Clive. The film culminates in a sequence on board Vail's new luxury liner *Princess Irene* as Irene and Paul return to France to clear his name. When Vail orders the captain to break the Atlantic speed record for crossing from America to France, the ship with 3,000 people on board goes at full speed through the fog and hits an iceberg. The finale is a precise re-creation of the *Titanic* disaster in miniature. The temperature falls, ice warnings are ignored, the iceberg is spotted, the ship collides with it, the watertight doors are closed. While the wireless operator desperately transmits SOS messages, the women and children are loaded into the lifeboats which are insufficient in number to accommodate all those on board. There are tearful partings and men demanding places in lifeboats and being refused. Irene refuses to leave Paul and they enjoy what they think will be their last moments together. Passengers and crew in the lounge gather round the piano to sing 'Nearer, My God, to Thee'. In Paris, Vail when he hears on the radio the news of the collision, which is declared the greatest maritime disaster since the *Titanic*, confesses to the murder and commits suicide. But this being Hollywood fiction, the bulkheads hold and the captain announces to the relieved passengers that help is on its way and they will all be saved.

Despite the happy ending, audiences could not fail to recognize the allusions to the real-life *Titanic* disaster. Also in 1937 David O. Selznick, whose plans were never less than grandiose, conceived the idea of a full-length *Titanic* feature. He engaged Alfred Hitchcock as director and proposed to purchase the derelict liner *Leviathan*, have it towed from New Jersey to California, shoot the film on board and then sink it. But the threat of a lawsuit from Howard Hughes, who had already registered the title *Titanic* and purchased an original screenplay on the subject, the expense of acquiring and transporting the *Leviathan* (which in the event was towed to Rosyth and broken up in 1938), protests from the British Chamber of Shipping and the Board of Trade to the American Ambassador in London about the reviving of the *Titanic* disaster story and finally the outbreak of war in Europe combined to scupper the project. Selznick transferred his attention to Daphne du Maurier's best-selling novel *Rebecca* which became Hitchcock's first American directorial assignment.[30]

The Germans were fascinated by the *Titanic* disaster and the lavishly staged *Titanic* (1943) was their third retelling of the story, following *Night and Ice* (1912) and the German version of *Atlantic* (1929). The idea for the film came from Dr Joseph Goebbels, the German propaganda minister, who had been plundering British history for film stories to emphasize the tyranny and corruption of the British. There was little real hatred of the British in pre-war Germany – the French were far more unpopular because of the Versailles Treaty and the French occupation of the Rhineland and Saarland – and the Germans had a romanticized view of England, fed by the popularity of English detective stories (particularly those of Edgar Wallace and Conan Doyle) and drawing-room comedies. The Nazis saw the English as a Nordic race and Hitler admired the British Empire. After 1939, a programme of anti-British propaganda was instituted in which Britain was denounced as a backward, philistine country run by a decadent aristocracy and an exploitative plutocracy, and as a cruel and tyrannical Empire which oppressed decent free Aryan peoples like the Irish and the Boers.[31] The Nazi film industry had already come up with *Das Herz der Königin* (which depicted Mary, Queen of Scots, as the victim of English imperialism,) *Ohm Krüger* (a pro-Boer version of the Boer War) and *Mein Leben für Irland* (a celebration of the heroic Irish resistance to the British Empire). Goebbels clearly relished the idea of the contemporary analogy suggested by the greatest ship afloat sinking as a result of British stupidity and greed. The script was written by a fanatical Nazi, Walter Zerlett-Olfenius, from a screen story by Harald Bratt and the direction was entrusted to Herbert Selpin. Selpin was known to have little love for the Nazi regime but he was an accomplished director of large-scale historical epics, which had included a previous maritime historical drama, the story of the inventor of the submarine Wilhelm Bauer, *Geheimakte WB I* (*Secret Paper WB I*; 1941).

The cast of characters included a number of historically verifiable figures (Bruce Ismay, Captain Smith, officers Murdoch and Lightoller, wireless operators Phillips and Bride, John Jacob Astor and his wife Madeleine) and verifiable incidents (the shortage of lifeboats, the lack of red distress flares, the *Californian* ignoring the warnings). But beyond that, the script adopted the *Grand Hotel* format which had structured *Atlantic*, a film which would have been familiar to German filmmakers as the first German talkie.

Selpin's film has rival financiers scheming to gain control of the White Star Line, two burgeoning love affairs, and an international jewel thief pursued by the ship's detective. But there is a strong and consistent propaganda line in the construction of the characters and events. The film was handsomely and lavishly staged, with an impressive *Titanic* model ship. The scenes of the disaster were well handled and the flooding of the engine rooms so effective that some shots were incorporated in *A Night to Remember*. The flooding of the first-class dining room, on the other hand, looks very obviously model work.

The whole disaster is laid squarely at the door of the aristocratic British capitalists, portrayed as impeccably dressed and ruthlessly acquisitive robber barons. This is in line with Nazi propaganda against British plutocrats and aristocrats as the precipitators of the war. To underline the point Bruce Ismay is given a title he never possessed and becomes Sir Bruce Ismay. No mention is made of the fact that John Jacob Astor, the richest man on board, is American and he is acted as if he were another of those icy, calculating British aristocrats. The official programme for the film refers to John Jacob and Madeleine as Lord and Lady Astor.[32] Although in the film these titles are not used, the implication of the characterizations is clear.

The film opens in the boardroom of the White Star Line where the company president, Ismay, announces that they have sustained heavy losses during the building of the *Titanic*. After the directors have left, however, he informs a few cronies that his plan is to force down the shares and then make a killing when the *Titanic* wins the Blue Riband for the fastest crossing of the Atlantic and the shares rise. His cronies join him on the ship and they further their plan by ordering the captain to take the ship at full speed. But his plan goes awry for, while they are aboard, the shares continue to fall and it is clear someone is working against him. That someone is Astor, who plans to gain control of the White Star Line and the *Titanic*, to further his ultimate aim – power. Their rivalry, conducted by telegrams to New York, continues throughout the voyage and is the reason, despite the ice warnings, that Ismay forbids the slackening of speed, thereby precipitating the disaster.

Greed goes hand in hand with immorality. Ismay, despite the presence on board of his mistress Gloria, plans to seduce wealthy Baltic German Sigrid Olinsky in order to use her money in his stock exchange deals. Astor, who has neglected his wife in pursuit of his business deals, suspects her of being unfaithful to him with the penniless aristocrat Lord Archibald Douglas, also on board. Douglas is interested in seducing Madeleine but she resists. Only at the end does Astor realize that his suspicions have been unfounded. But by now, his schemes are in ruins and his own life forfeit. Madeleine leaves for the lifeboat. Compounding greed and immorality is cowardice. Ismay, Astor and the White Star directors all desperately offer money for places in the lifeboats. But Ismay is the only one to get into a lifeboat, conducted there by Officer Petersen who wants to ensure that he survives to be punished. Previously, Gloria has abandoned Ismay to save herself.

By contrast with the British villains, most of the virtuous people on board are German. Petersen, the First Officer, is German. He is the only man to sense the approaching danger, warning constantly about icebergs, denouncing and defying Ismay and, at the end, rescuing a little girl and swimming with her to safety on a lifeboat. In this, he directly emulates the British Second Officer, Lanchester, in *Atlantic*. He falls in love with Sigrid Olinsky, the wealthy Baltic German woman who learns during the course of the voyage that she has lost her fortune with the confiscation of her Russian estates. The realization turns her from a social butterfly into a heroine. She too fulfils a propaganda function, the reinforcement of Nazi gender stereotypes. Dressed in the officer's overcoat Petersen gives her, she helps women and children into the boats and then when ordered to join them, although unwilling, obeys orders and does so, like a 'good German'. She is later united with Petersen, who survives.

A direct contrast with the blue bloods is the other romance, a tender and innocent romance between a poor but honest German couple, manicurist Heidi and the first violinist in the orchestra, Franz Gruber. As the ship sinks, he puts her in a lifeboat. But he too will be saved. Also German are immigrants Jan and Anna, an idealized Germanic rural couple, devoted to each other, who are separated in the panic. They survive and are reunited in the court room at the inquiry. Finally there are the poor but brilliant scientist Professor Bergmann and his assistant, Dr Lawrence. Bergmann has finally solved his life's work in a set of calculations and, when the ship sinks, he gives them to Lawrence and urges him to get them to the world; he has lived his life, so he stays behind. The Germans all behave with honour, decency and stoicism.

Selpin is the first *Titanic* director to make a significant point about the class difference. He demonstrates the privileged nature of the first-class passenger list and at the same time introduces the *dramatis personae* in the first scene on board the ship when the principal characters sweep down the grand staircase into the dining room, each in turn identified and commented on by a group of the ship's officers. They include John Jacob Astor, the richest man in the world, and his wife; Sigrid Olinsky, the wealthy Baltic German; Lord Archibald Douglas; Sir Bruce Ismay and his glamorous mistress Gloria; Cristobal Mendoz, the Cuban jewel thief; and lastly Professor Bergmann and his assistant Lawrence, who are dismissed by the officers as being both German and penniless and therefore of no account. Significantly there are no Americans in the film, because the British are the villains.

Selpin also includes several scenes in steerage full of immigrants. The class contrast is forcibly stressed when the ship's engines stop and the third-class passengers march under Jan's leadership out of steerage and into the first-class ballroom, and stare about them in amazement at the pomp and luxury. It is a scene strongly reminiscent of the intrusion of the beggars into the coronation ceremonies in G. W. Pabst's film of the Brecht–Weill *Threepenny Opera* (1931), which was also anxious to make a point about class conflict in British society. But there is a racial message as well as a class message in the steerage scenes. Along with the decent Germans Jan and Anna there are two English friends Bobby and Henry who are set against each other by the wanton and voluptuous gypsy girl, Marcia, who does a lascivious dance which embarrasses Anna, and whose provocation of the friends causes them to fight. As a result Bobby ends up in the brig, along with Mendoz who has been apprehended stealing Mrs Astor's jewels. Matters are made worse by a character billed as a Levantine – to be understood by contemporary audiences as a Jew. He slips a knife to Bobby, almost causing Henry to be knifed. Later when the crew separate the women and children from the men, to distribute the lifejackets, he stimulates a riot, which leads to the men breaking out and killing the officer after he has fired at them. When the ship begins to sink, Henry breaks Bobby and Mendoz out of the brig. Bobby, Henry and Franz Gruber improvise a raft and escape on it with Anna, now separated from Jan. Mendoz fights the Levantine for a lifeboat place and they both fall on to a boat containing Marcia, causing it to crash into the water. So the only Latin in the film is the self-serving Cuban jewel thief; the gypsy causes trouble and is last seen fleeing with the Jew, also a malign influence.

The final sequence of the film, the court of inquiry, attended by Petersen and Sigrid, underlines the propaganda message. Ismay is acquitted of all blame and the responsibility is laid on Captain Smith, who has gone down with the ship, and who throughout had been overruled and dictated to by Ismay. Petersen is disgusted and the final titles remind the audience that British greed was responsible for the deaths of 1,500 innocent people who remain unavenged. The clear implication is that Germany is now doing that avenging.

The propaganda intent ruled out Captain Smith's 'Be British' injunction and Guggenheim's 'We shall go down like gentlemen', though Ismay declares the ship unsinkable. Nevertheless Selpin did evoke sympathy for passengers in their final crisis: the Duchess of Canterville who had had a foreboding of disaster standing at the rail and lowering her head resignedly as the last lifeboat casts off leaving her behind; wireless operator Phillips remaining at his post to the end but freeing his canary from its cage as 'Nearer, My God, to Thee' is played by the band, who have stayed on deck playing Germanic marches (rather than the authentic transatlantic ragtime).

Selpin himself also became a victim of the tragedy. While shooting the film's interiors at Tobis Studios in Berlin in May 1942, he sent Zerlett-Olfenius to Gotenhafen (now Gdynia) with a second unit to shoot footage on board the liner *Cap Ancona* for incorporation into the film. Annoyed at the lack of progress, Selpin went there himself in July and in the course of a quarrel about the co-operation of the German navy made various insulting remarks about the armed forces. The fanatical Nazi Zerlett-Olfenius immediately reported him to the authorities and he was arrested and imprisoned on a charge of treason. He was found hanged in his cell on 31 July 1942. Suicide was the verdict but it was widely believed that he had been liquidated by the Gestapo on Goebbels' orders.[33] Director Werner Klingler (whose wife Liselott was playing Anna in the film) was brought in to complete the shooting.

Although the film had been awarded the classification *staatspolitisch wertvoll* (of political merit) and *künstlerisch wertvoll* (of artistic merit), when Goebbels saw the completed film, he decided it could not be released in Germany. The scenes of panic among the passengers as disaster struck were uncomfortably reminiscent of the reaction of German civilians to the Allied bombing. Even more important, in the context of Nazi cinema, the Führer figure Ismay was shown as corrupt and self-seeking and responsible for the deaths of hundreds of people. This portrait came too close to home for comfort. To recoup part of the enormous cost of the film, Goebbels had it released in neutral and occupied countries. It opened in Paris in November 1943 and became the most popular German film shown in occupied France. It was not shown in Germany until after the war. In 1949 a German distributor Sud-Verleih acquired a print of *Titanic* and received permission from the new German censorship authority, FSK, to exhibit it in the French and American zones of occupied Germany. But in 1950 the British requested withdrawal of this permission to exhibit on the grounds that the film was 'harmful to Allied prestige', specifically that it was anti-British propaganda. It was not withdrawn but the final inquiry scene which indicted the British authorities for covering up the truth of the disaster and the anti-British end-title were cut and the film was given permission by FSK for showing throughout the Federal Republic of Germany.

On 20 March 1950, the *Daily Express* broke the story in Britain that Goebbels' 'hate the British masterpiece' was being shown in Germany to large and enthusiastic audiences. The story was picked up by most of the other British newspapers and pressure mounted on the government to demand a ban. By this time, *Titanic* had received its German première in Stuttgart on 7 February 1950, with six of the original cast present, and had been shown with success in Frankfurt, Nuremberg and Munich. But British pressure paid off and the film was banned on 1 April 1950. The ban did not affect communist East Germany, where the film's anti-British bias suited the authorities very well. The ban in the West lasted until Allied occupation came to an end in 1955. Thereafter *Titanic* was shown in cinemas and on television and is currently available (still without the final inquiry scene) on video as a golden age classic.[34]

Hollywood finally came up with its *Titanic* in 1953. Why was the 1950s so interested in the story? It was an age of anxiety. The war had ended in 1945 but the atomic bomb created fear of universal destruction, enhanced when the hydrogen bomb was tested in 1954. In Sir Winston Churchill's words, an 'Iron Curtain' had descended across Europe and a Cold War had begun between the democratic West and the communist East. The People's Republic of China was created by Mao Tse-Tung in 1949 and signed a thirty-year pact with Russia in 1950. The Berlin blockade (1948–49), the Korean War (1950–53), the creation of the Warsaw Pact (1955), and the suppression of the Hungarian uprising (1956) all served to underline the menace of communism to the free world. National paranoia was fed by the McCarthyite purge in the US and the operations of the House Un-American Activities Committee; the arrest and execution of the Rosenbergs for espionage; and the defection of Burgess and Maclean from Britain to the USSR. In Britain, the empire was beginning to crumble, with independence for India in 1947 followed by the beginning of disengagement from Africa with Ghana gaining independence in 1957, while nationalist uprisings in Kenya, Malaya and Cyprus and the failed Suez operation all confirmed Britain's decline from world power status. The *Titanic* story became a metaphor for the destruction of a secure pre-war world. Much closer to the Nazi *Titanic* in approach than to the subsequent British *A Night to Remember*, 20th Century-Fox's *Titanic* was expensively produced and lavishly mounted, sensitively directed, skilfully edited and handsomely photographed. It was entirely shot in the studio and the studio tank, utilizing a 28-foot model of the ship and excellent special effects from the team headed by Ray Kellogg. They did, however, perpetrate a fundamental error: the iceberg strikes the ship on the port side, whereas in reality it was on the starboard side. The director Jean Negulesco, who shot no scenes at all actually at sea, was fully aware of the importance of the special effects and constantly adapted his shooting schedule to meet the demands of his special effects team.[35]

Interestingly he chose to tackle the story in a similar way to Selpin, reflecting the fact that the audience would know that disaster was to be the climax of the film. Negulesco recalled: 'Since the audience would be anticipating a catastrophic climax right from the beginning of the picture, I wanted to make the build-up, the preliminaries, as gay and light as possible, without hints of darkness; I wanted to play against the climax.'[36] Herbert Selpin seems to have had much the same idea. His widow told David Stewart Hull that he greeted the project with enthusiasm for 'the lighter elements of the first part of the voyage would gradually give way to the suspense and danger and final tragedy, a most appealing progression'.[37]

Fox's *Titanic* cost $1,805,000 to produce, making it one of their six costliest productions of the year.[38] The Charles Brackett–Walter Reisch–

Richard Breen screenplay, which was to win an Oscar, adopted the *Grand Hotel* format. *Titanic*, which featured seven stars (Clifton Webb, Barbara Stanwyck, Robert Wagner, Audrey Dalton, Thelma Ritter, Brian Aherne and Richard Basehart) needs to be judged more as high-quality melodrama than as documentary reconstruction, though in the event it was the factual scenes that were to elicit critical approval. The opening titles announce that all navigational details and conversations are taken verbatim from inquiries held by the US Congress and the British Board of Trade. Among the crew and passengers are a number of historical characters: of the crew, Captain Smith, Chief Officer Wilde, First Officer Murdoch, Second Officer Lightoller, wireless officers Bride and Phillips appear, and of the passengers, John Jacob Astor, and his wife Madeleine, Mr and Mrs Isidor Straus, George Widener and (as a one-line bit part) Benjamin Guggenheim. The Countess of Rothes, Lady Duff Gordon and Major Archie Butt are mentioned but not seen. White Star Line director Harold Sanderson is seen at the beginning. Several historical characters are inexplicably renamed: the tough, forthright, wisecracking Montana mining millionairess Maude Young is clearly the 'Unsinkable' Molly Brown, bandmaster McDermott is Wallace Hartley and lookout Devlin is Frederick Fleet. The elements of the myth are carefully reproduced: the Anglo-Saxon stoicism and chivalry, the affirmation of Christian faith, 'Nearer, My God, to Thee'. There is no panic and the story is one of nobility, self-sacrifice and tearful partings.

The filming of the disaster had a powerful effect on Barbara Stanwyck, who recalled:

> The night we were making the scene of the dying ship in the outdoor tank at Twentieth, it was bitter cold. I was forty-seven feet up in the air in a lifeboat. The water below was agitated into a heaving, rolling mass and it was thick with other lifeboats full of women and children. I looked up at the faces lined along the rail – those left behind to die with the ship. I thought of the men and women who had been through this thing in our time. We were recreating an actual tragedy and I burst into tears. I shook with great racking sobs and couldn't stop![39]

Like Selpin's *Titanic*, this 1953 Hollywood version has a powerful propaganda message. It is a *Titanic* for the Cold War. First of all, in addition to stressing Anglo-Saxon chivalry and stoicism, it stresses America and Americanism in contradistinction to the Old World. The central plotline has Julia Sturges returning from Europe with her two children, essentially running away from her wealthy socialite husband

and the rootless cosmopolitan existence they have led and from an arranged marriage with a Metternich for her daughter Annette, who is becoming a spoiled, affected prig. 'I've seen a great many international marriages and I've never seen a happy one,' Julia observes. She wants to bring up Annette and her son Norman as ordinary decent healthy Americans ('We're Americans – we belong in America'). Her husband, Richard Ward Sturges, pursues her and manages to get aboard the ship by buying a third-class ticket from a Basque immigrant. The conflict and contrast between Julia and Richard is effectively drawn, and well played by Stanwyck and Webb in characteristic roles. She, down-to-earth, all-American, humble born, simple and sincere, longs for her small-town Michigan home and rejects her rootless European life; he, brittle, snobbish and cosmopolitan, the best dressed man of his genera-tion, prefers the aristocratic life of the Old World. He is depicted as a friend of the Astors, the Wideners and the Strauses. He tries to persuade her to stay with him, and when she refuses, threatens to take the children from her. She retaliates by telling him that he may be able to get Annette back, but Norman is not his son. He is the product of a fleeting affair she had entered into in her unhappiness as Richard had killed her love for him by mocking her gaucherie and forcing her into an alien way of life. As a result, Richard brutally rejects Norman, the son who adores him. However, when the disaster strikes, Richard realizes the foolishness of his attitude and the futility of his lifestyle. He and Julia rediscover their love and renew their vows before she and Annette are put into a boat. Norman leaves the boat, giving up his seat to an old lady, and rejoins his father, who expresses his love for and pride in him; they will go down together on the ship.

The main narrative line thus stresses the unity and sanctity of the American family, redeemed and re-established at the end. It is underlined by the authentic vignette in which Mrs Straus refuses to leave her husband, saying she had lived with him for forty years and would stay with him. The 1950s was very much the decade of the idealized American family, particularly in long-running television sitcoms such as *Father Knows Best*, *The Aldrich Family* and *The Adventures of Ozzie and Harriet*, and *Titanic* conforms precisely to that ideal.

The message is reinforced by the sub-plot involving Annette. Initially anxious to return to Europe with her father, she meets on the voyage and falls for clean-cut all-American college boy Giff Rogers from Indiana, returning with his Purdue college tennis team from playing against Oxford University. He romances Annette and succeeds in knocking all the affected European nonsense out of her. This is coded symbolically by his teaching her an American dance (Navaho Rag) and singing American college songs ('Amherst', 'Cornell'). He survives after being knocked unconscious when he falls into a lifeboat while freeing it when the ropes get tangled, and clearly he and Annette will be united as the perfect American couple in America, making a success of their lives where the older generation had failed.

The second continuing theme of the film is the importance of religion. Significantly the film was known in production as *Nearer, My God, to Thee* and the title was changed to *Titanic* only when shooting was completed.[40] In this it is part of a 1950s cinematic trend. This is the era of the godless Soviet Union which is criticized implicitly in large-scale biblical epics that contrast democratic Christianity or Judaism with totalitarian pagan empires (*Quo Vadis*, *The Robe*, *The Ten Commandments*, *Ben-Hur*) and explicitly in straightforward anti-communist propaganda such as *Red Planet Mars* (1952), in which the voice of God speaks from Mars, sparking a worldwide Christian revival, endorsed by the US President, which results in the toppling of the Soviet regime. *Titanic* includes a church service on board, conducted by the captain, attended by the crew and many of the leading characters, and including prayers and the singing of 'Holy, Holy, Holy, Lord God Almighty'. It also features among the characters Revd George Healey, a Roman Catholic priest defrocked for alcoholism, and returning to face his Boston family. He redeems himself by going below to deliver the last rites to injured crewmen as the ship sinks and he goes down with it. The emotional climax of the film sees the entire crew and the male passengers, including Straus, Astor, Richard and Norman Sturges, standing and singing 'Nearer, My God, to Thee'. The ship sinks but the hymn is heard again on the soundtrack as the lifeboats pull away and the final narration is spoken (by an uncredited Michael Rennie).

Of the elements of the myth, Anglo-Saxon stoicism is to the fore, with no panic and only one first-class passenger (the odious social climber Earl Meeker) escaping disguised as a woman. In reality, it was an eighteen-year-old third-class passenger Daniel Buckley who did this, though there were persistent but unsubstantiated rumours of a first-class passenger behaving similarly. The Strauses stay together. The Astors part as John Jacob puts his wife into a lifeboat and steps back. The first use of SOS is included. But there is no injunction from the captain to 'be British' and no Guggenheim saying, 'We've dressed in our best and are prepared to go down like gentlemen.'

This is not essentially a film about class. All the leading characters are travelling first-class and most of them behave well. There are only two scenes in steerage, one with the obligatory singing and dancing, and the steerage passengers are mainly Latins and not as in later versions Irish. The scenes in steerage are there for plot purposes. Sturges came aboard with the Basque family, having bought the father's ticket, and he goes back for them when disaster strikes and gets them into a lifeboat, reinforcing his chivalrous attitude.

This is very much an American version of the tragedy. There are no British passengers. The crew, however, are British and so is the ship. This is emphasized by the playing of British tunes ('The British Grenadiers', 'Rule Britannia') as the ship leaves Cherbourg. There is no particular desire to vilify the British. J. Bruce Ismay, Captain Lord and Thomas Andrews do not appear in the film. The delayed ice warnings, the shortage of lifeboats and the lack of binoculars are mentioned. But Sanderson, the company representative, is seen saying that while the company would appreciate a record crossing, the captain must exercise prudence. Nevertheless, one cannot escape the feeling that it is a disaster to a British ship which sinks the Americans. As the *Titanic* leaves Cherbourg, Captain Smith receives from the captain of the first ship on which he served a faded and tattered ensign. He orders it hoisted and the last shots of Captain Smith have him looking up sadly at the tattered ensign, a symbol of the fading glories of the British Empire, whose world-role is now in the 1950s being assumed by the United States. The scene of the captain sitting smilingly watching the American college boys singing their songs similarly suggests that the power is passing from an Old World empire to the young democracy of the New World, with the blessing of their NATO ally.

The film netted in domestic rentals $2,250,000, making it Fox's sixth biggest grossing film of the year after *The Robe, How to Marry a Millionaire, Gentlemen Prefer Blondes, Call Me Madam* and *Niagara*.[41] What Steven Biel wrote of the coverage in 1912 could apply equally to the 1953 film: 'Part Christian conversion narrative and part knightly adventure, the conventional version of the disaster provided closure by showing how the ruling class redeemed itself when put to the test and, more broadly, how modernity was traditional after all.'[42]

TWO
The Making of the Film

The idea of filming Walter Lord's book originated with producer William MacQuitty. MacQuitty had been born in Belfast in 1905 and the *Titanic* had loomed large in his young life. He had watched it being built at the Harland and Wolff shipyard and at the age of six had been taken by his father to the launch on 31 May 1911. He felt great affinity with the ship. His own birthday was in May and he saw the ship as representing his chance to leave Belfast and travel the world. He recalled the ship's trials on Belfast Lough, its departure on its maiden voyage and the huge impact of the disaster on the Ulster community.[1] The idea of the *Titanic* and its tragedy remained with him during what became an adventurous career as banker in China, soldier in India and farmer in Ireland. He entered the film industry during the war, making documentary films for the Ministry of Information, and afterwards established himself as a producer in the commercial industry. In 1956 MacQuitty's wife Betty drew his attention to Walter Lord's new book *A Night to Remember*. Like MacQuitty, Lord, who worked for a New York advertising agency, was fascinated by the *Titanic* tragedy and had devoted years to assembling an accurate account based in part on documentary sources and in part on interviews and correspondence with the survivors. First published in New York and later in London, the book became an instant bestseller. MacQuitty took an option on the film rights to the book for £5,000 and the promise of a small percentage of the profits.[2] He took the project to John Davis, managing director of the Rank Organization. Davis was initially sceptical of both the project and MacQuitty's intended approach of documentary authenticity, telling him: 'It's just another shipwreck, it's been done before, it's small screen black and white, you have no stars in it and it's going to be costly.'[3] Davis had some justification for his reservations. After all, the Hollywood company 20th Century-Fox had released its star-studded version of the story, *Titanic*, only three years earlier. The film would turn out to be Rank's most expensive production and it would suffer in America because of its lack of star names. But MacQuitty stood his ground and argued that it was more than just a shipwreck story, it was a prestige project about the end of an era, an era of privilege and class arrogance, epitomized in the *Titanic* memorial in Belfast that listed the names of the victims in order of importance, while the Great War memorial next to it listed them in alphabetical order. It was envisaged as a film on an epic scale and Rank was embarking on its last big push for international success with a series of expensive epics which would include *Campbell's Kingdom* (1957), *Windom's Way* (1958), *Northwest Frontier* (1959) and *Ferry to Hong Kong* (1959).

In 1956 Rank had announced a policy of only producing films with 'international entertainment appeal' that would be 'vigorously sold in foreign markets'. In 1957 Rank Film Distributors of America (RFDA) was set up with the aim of bypassing the American distributors and reaching the American audience directly. But in 1959, after only eighteen months, RFDA was closed down with reportedly heavy losses.[4]

Davis gave MacQuitty the go-ahead. Interestingly, both MacQuitty and director Roy Baker expressed admiration for John Davis, one of the most feared and hated men in British cinema. MacQuitty found him 'straight and he kept his word', and Baker thought he had 'drive and ambition and he was capable of keeping Rank on an even keel with all its ramifications'.[5] He certainly displayed those qualities in backing *A Night to Remember*. The film, expected to run for 113 minutes, was budgeted at a cost of £499,670. It was an enormous sum for the British film industry in those days. Eventually, the film's length extended to 123 minutes and the cost to £530,000, though the *Sunday Dispatch* reported a rumour that it had actually risen to £600,000.[6] Of this, £45,000 went on the construction of a scale model of the *Titanic*, on a scale of one in ten.[7]

MacQuitty assembled his production team. The film was to be directed by Rank contract director Roy Baker. MacQuitty thought Baker as a director 'absolutely splendid. He would only do subjects he believed in and he believed in this. He had enormous contact with everyone and kept the actors happy and in balance. He was tireless. He had a great sense of period.'[8] Baker welcomed the project. He was attracted by 'the size of it ... the chance to make a film of real substance ... it was a golden opportunity to make a film about something important'.[9] It was Baker who suggested Eric Ambler as scriptwriter. They had already worked together on several films and Baker commented, 'We developed a long-lasting friendship, and of course one thing about Eric is that he

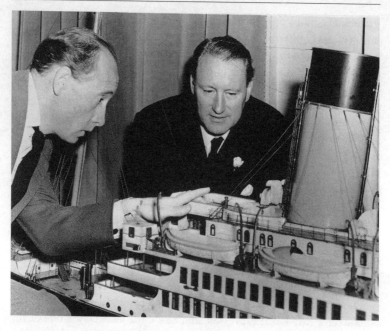

1. *Producer William MacQuitty and director Roy Baker inspect the scale model of the* Titanic.

presents you with a script which is beautifully finished in every detail.'[10] MacQuitty thought the script 'superb' but Ambler modestly declared, 'Everything was in the book. All I had to do was knit it together.'[11] Ambler's first draft script was completed by September 1956, a second draft by March 1957 and the final version by August 1957. It was vetted for historical accuracy by Walter Lord.

The rest of the team that MacQuitty assembled were regular collaborators of Roy Baker, people in whose judgement and quality he had absolute faith. His cameraman was Geoffrey Unsworth, who had photographed three of Baker's recent films, *Passage Home* (1954), *Jacqueline* (1956) and *Tiger in the Smoke* (1956), as well as MacQuitty's *The Black Tent* (1956). Baker recalled: 'He was just great ... We struck up a firm friendship, and a sympathetic and responsive working relationship.'[12] The art director was Alex Vetchinsky, known as 'Vetch', who had been in films since 1928 and whose atmospheric sets had enhanced many notable British films. He had handled the art direction on Roy Baker's films *The October Man*, *The Weaker Sex*, *Highly Dangerous*, *Morning Departure* and *Passage Home*. MacQuitty described him as 'an impatient perfectionist' and this perfectionism would lead to the meticulous re-creation of the *Titanic* interiors.[13] *A Night to Remember* was the only film in production at Pinewood at the time and all 1,200 of the studio's work force were involved in it.

The score was in the hands of William Alwyn, one of the finest of British film composers. For Baker he had already scored *The October Man*, *The House on the Square* and *Morning Departure*. Baker recalled Alwyn as 'one of the people I am proud to have worked with. Quiet, sensitive and wonderfully responsive to the style of the film and the varying moods of the scenes within it – and in complete command of the means of expressing them.'[14]

The rest of the production team were experienced professionals. Baker and MacQuitty were full of praise for the special effects unit headed by Bill Warrington with Skeets Kelly as cameraman. 'They performed miracles with the techniques that were available to them at that time,' said Baker. Warrington later told MacQuitty, 'he had never enjoyed his work so much as he had on this film'. Baker also recalled with admiration production manager Jack Hanbury ('unflappable and urbane … a joy to work with'), editor Sidney Hayers ('His final edit of the film was excellent') and costume designer Yvonne Caffin ('Throughout the film Yvonne's presentation of ninety-two speaking parts was perfect and made an enormous contribution to the final effect').[15] Baker concluded: 'If ever a picture was a team effort *A Night to Remember* was the example … I owe them all a great debt for their unstinting support. There is no doubt they were inspired by the subject. It was punishingly hard work but they took it in their stride.'[16]

Before shooting began, Baker and MacQuitty viewed all the previous versions of the story. Baker thought the 1929 *Atlantic* and the 1953 *Titanic* 'romantic fantasies' using the *Titanic* merely as background (he had the same view of the 1997 *Titanic*). The 1943 *Titanic* he thought 'okay but it was a sheer piece of propaganda'. He admired the fact that the film used a real liner for some of the scenes and shot sequences on location in the Baltic.[17] It was good enough for four shots from it (two of the ship at sea; two of the engine room flooding) to be incorporated into *A Night to Remember*.

From the outset, the watchword of Baker and MacQuitty was 'authenticity'.[18] The poster promoting the film was to proclaim in capital letters 'As It Really Happened'. Unlike the previous sound film versions, this was not to be a romantic melodrama; it would be a docu-drama. Although the distributors had wanted the film shot in Vistavision and

Technicolor, MacQuitty insisted on black and white to enable him to use available library footage to obtain the appropriate period feel. Baker recalled the exhaustive historical research that underlay the script:

> There was a considerable amount of historical evidence, mostly un-disputed but some of it questionable, all of it to be sifted. There were a number of myths and fantasies which had to be carefully evaluated. There were reports of two inquiries, one by the U.S. Congress and the other by the British Board of Trade. Any survivors within reach were asked for their experiences and comments. We had considerable help from Commander Charles Lightoller's family. All this ground had been thoroughly scrutinized by Walter Lord and his book was the basis of all our work. All the information was triple-distilled by Eric Ambler, who wrote the script. The balance that he achieved between the many disparate elements was superb, bearing in mind that it had to be compressed into a reasonable length for a film.[19]

The interiors and exteriors of the ship were based on contemporary plans and illustrations of the *Titanic*. Bound into Baker's copy of the script are the designs for the ship reproduced from a 1911 issue of *The Shipbuilder*, and charts showing who was in which lifeboat. He recalled that: 'All the settings were faithful reproductions of the originals', re-created by Vetchinsky and his assistants. 'Their scrupulous attention to detail brought the whole thing to life. The grand staircase was marvellous and the first-class dining-room was exactly like the original.'[20] These interiors had to be constructed on platforms supported by hydraulic lifts so that they could be tilted for the flooding scenes. The sounds made by the hydraulic lifts were incorporated into the film as the creaks and groans of the dying ship.

A 300-foot section of the port side of the *Titanic*, with promenade deck, boat deck, two funnels and four lifeboats, was constructed on a base of four acres of concrete in a field at Pinewood Studios by Vetchinsky and his team.[21] MacQuitty purchased lifeboats identical to those on the *Titanic* from the liner *Franconia*, then being broken up in Scotland. An exact replica of the lifeboat which Lightoller commanded was built by the Thames boatyard of Lightoller's son, Colonel R. T. Lightoller.[22] During the scene of lunch at the captain's table on the last day, the same menu was served as had been eaten by the captain's guests. Baker says: 'There was no need to do this, but some food had to be eaten and it might as well be correct. It all helped the atmosphere, which ... helped the actors.'[23]

The desire for authenticity went even further. Baker and Muir Mathieson, the musical director, agreed that there would be no music, apart from that performed by the ship's orchestra, until the plunge. After the credits, apart from a snatch of music over the date, there is no background music until the captain orders the guns broken out and steerage passengers begin to panic.

Even Walter Lord's encyclopaedic research was not infallible. He had recorded that the painting hanging in the first-class smoking room was of New York Harbor and called 'The Approach to the New World'. This was faithfully reproduced for the film and after completion it was presented by the Rank Organization to Lord. Lord subsequently discovered that this painting had hung in the *Titanic*'s sister ship *Olympic* and it was a painting of Plymouth Harbour that hung in the *Titanic*.[24]

In addition to Walter Lord's research and advice, the production drew on a wide variety of other advisers. Joseph Boxhall, fourth officer on the *Titanic*, and Captain Harry Grattidge, formerly captain of the *Queen Mary*, were the film's technical advisers. MacQuitty corresponded with fifty of the eighty-five survivors still alive in 1957. Several of them watched the filming, and gave advice on detail, notably Edith Russell and Lawrence Beesley, who had written his own book about his experiences on the *Titanic*. Captain Smith's daughter Mrs Helen Russell-Cooke visited the set and was overcome with emotion on meeting Laurence Naismith, who was playing her father and who was said to resemble him closely. Survivor Eva Hart could not bring herself to watch the filming but attended the première and wrote to MacQuitty to say 'The film itself was so realistic and so well produced that, even from my own experience I was unable to fault anything about it.' Joseph Boxhall wept when he saw the finished film and declared it 'terribly right'.[25]

There was one survivor who was not entirely satisfied and that was stewardess Violet Jessop who in a private letter dated 29 July 1958 wrote:

> I think Pinewood did a wonderful job in recreating something that happened so long ago and if I disagree with a lot of things – such as the scene where it would appear the third-class were locked in, and the behaviour of some of the crew – it is only because to a person like myself who was there it seems like undue criticism. I now greatly regret not having accepted Mr. MacQuitty's several invitations; if I had seen some of the sequences, I could have pointed out discrepancies. I begged Miss Coffin [the costume designer Yvonne Caffin] when she interviewed me ... not to put women on board in the very beflowered, beplumed

2. *Great pains were taken to cast actors who resembled the historical originals: Captain E. J. Smith (left) and Laurence Naismith as Smith (right).*

hats of the period as American women (and they were mostly Americans) would never wear street hats on board, and look what met your eyes at the Captain's table! Everything except the kitchen stove on their heads![26]

There was a large cast: ninety-two speaking parts and some 1,500 extras. Great pains were taken to select actors who resembled the historical characters they were playing. The speaking parts were filled mainly by English character actors, though MacQuitty ensured that there was a representative contingent of Irish (Richard Hayward, Bee Duffell, Harold Goldblatt and Joseph Tomelty, among them). Baker secured the services of many actors he had worked with before – 'my rep', he called them – among them Michael Goodliffe as Thomas Andrews and Laurence Naismith as Captain Smith. Naismith had spent two years at sea as a cabin boy and, conscious of the responsibility of playing a person whom many still remembered, researched the part extensively.[27] Baker recalled: 'Michael Goodliffe was a great favourite of mine. Laurence

Naismith was also in several things I did, as were Sam Kydd, Victor Maddern and quite a few others. Those were reliable people and they fitted in so easily and so well.'[28] Laurence Naismith, Thomas Heathcote, Kenneth Griffith, Stratford Johns, Gerald Harper, Howard Lang and Philip Ray had all appeared in Baker's *Tiger in the Smoke* and Michael Goodliffe, Julian Somers, Alec McCowen, Norman Rossington, Stratford Johns and Glyn Houston had all appeared in his *The One That Got Away*. Baker accepted two members of the 'Rank Charm School' – Ronald Allen and Jill Dixon – to play the honeymoon couple and he thought 'they did it well'.[29] Honor Blackman and David McCallum were also Rank contract artists. For the most part the cast responded well to Roy Baker's direction. Kenneth Griffith thought him 'a fine director ... nice man, very underrated', and David McCallum thought him 'a wonderful director'.[30] The only one of his large cast who caused him any trouble was Tucker McGuire playing Molly Brown – the actress was 'ornery ... I don't know what got into her'.[31]

The absence of a star remained a major problem, however, and it was decided that a star should be sought to add box-office appeal. MacQuitty, Ambler and Baker all agreed that the only role which stood out in the ensemble cast was that of Second Officer Lightoller: 'It could be said to be the central character but it was not a star part: *primus inter pares* at best.'[32] They also agreed that the ideal casting would be Kenneth More. Baker flew to Bermuda where More was filming *The Admirable Crichton* and put the proposition to him. More, fascinated by the story, proved to be enthusiastic. He recalled: 'Although the *Titanic* would obviously be the star, I felt part of this ship, and agreed to play the part.'[33]

More was an excellent choice. He was familiar with the sea, having served as a lieutenant in the Royal Navy during the war, and had played several supporting roles as naval officers in films he made after the war (*Scott of the Antarctic*, *Morning Departure*). He had become a popular star in the comedy *Genevieve* (1953) and had consolidated his appeal as Douglas Bader in *Reach for the Sky* (1956), the top British box-office success of the year. His image of the bright and breezy 'never say die' Englishman appealed to 1950s audiences. Josh Billings reported in *Kinematograph Weekly* (12 December 1957) that More was 'unquestionably a big draw' and 'could turn an ordinary film into a box-office success mainly on the strength of his name.' And *A Night to Remember* was far from being an ordinary film. Rank were anxious to sign him and *A Night to Remember* became the first film made on a new contract with

Rank which saw him star in seven films in five years at a fee of £40,000 per film.[34] Lightoller's son advised More on how to play his father and Lightoller's widow visited the set to observe the filming.[35] Both Baker and MacQuitty were delighted with More's performance, although he played it without Lightoller's West Country accent which is revealed in a 1937 radio interview. MacQuitty thought him 'absolutely right' in the part and Baker thought More 'absolutely marvellous because he pulled the whole thing together … and he was very good at working with the other actors'.[36]

Shooting on the film began on 15 October 1957 and lasted until 4 March 1958. Half of this time was spent doing night shooting. The interiors and deck exteriors were shot at Pinewood and individual life-boat scenes were shot in the studio tank. It made life difficult for the actors. Honor Blackman recalled it being 'technically very difficult … jumping into boats and being on a tank in the studio'.[37] Most of the shots were taken from the port side; for the few scenes which needed to be on starboard, Baker shot on the port side through a mirror to reverse the image.

The studio tank was not big enough to encompass long-shots of the lifeboats and the passengers in the water. Many of these were taken on location at Ruislip Lido in freezing conditions between 15 and 23 October, where in the first scenes to be filmed 500 extras had to jump repeatedly into the icy water.[38] Kenneth More, who had to do the same, took the precaution of wearing a wetsuit under his uniform and fortifying himself with tots of neat rum.[39] The drenched extras were dried out in rooms equipped with machines that blew hot air. McCallum recalled:

> It was only about 10 degrees warmer than it was in the Atlantic on the actual night. The water was extremely cold and we didn't have wetsuits or anything like that … they were only allowed to have us in the water about five minutes at a time. Then they used to whip us out, take our clothes and put us in rooms with these great heaters.[40]

But the time and the location produced effective scenes, complete with the actors' breath on the frosty air.

Exterior long-shots of the lifeboats being lowered into the water from a real liner were needed to link the shots taken on the studio-constructed decks and the scenes of the lifeboats in the water. The Shaw Savill shipping line agreed to allow exterior scenes to be taken on one of their ships MV *Dominion Monarch* in the Royal Albert Dock but shortly before filming was due to begin permission was withdrawn. The matter, it seems, had come to the attention of the chairman of the line, Basil Sanderson. He was the son of Harold Sanderson, who had been chairman of the White Star Line between 1913 and 1927 and was himself married to the daughter of Bruce Ismay. He did not want the matter reopened. Neither did the rest of the shipping companies, all of which refused co-operation.[41] This compounded the decision of Sir Frederick Rebbeck, chairman of Harland and Wolff, who also refused any co-operation with the filmmakers. The company issued a statement deploring the fact that a film company was seeking to make money out of the tragedy. 'Too many people from this shipyard lost their lives that night and too many others as well. Why should we help to make an entertainment out of it.'[42] Clearly, for the shipbuilders and the shipping lines the subject was still a painful one and one which they preferred not to see revived.

However, MacQuitty managed to get permission from the firm of Ship Breaking Industries to film on the ancient steamship RMS *Asturias* which was waiting on the Clyde to be broken up. It was repainted in White Star Line colours by Glasgow art students. Stuntmen in costumes were paid £1 per foot to jump the eighty feet from deck to water. Editor Sidney Hayers was sent up with a second unit and filmed for ten nights.[43] Back at Pinewood, Baker carried on filming the main action. The furnaces in the engine room set had real coal fires in them, which at one stage set the floor alight, but the fire was rapidly put out. Supplementary scenes for the engine rooms were taken at Cricklewood pumping station, whose 1905 engines resembled those of the *Titanic*.

While principal filming was going on, the model work was being undertaken in the studio tank with full-length model ships, models of sections of the ship and electrically operated lifeboat models. The final scenes for the film to be shot were those of the departure of Sir Richard and his wife from their stately home. The finished film was then scored, cut, dubbed and prepared for release. Kenneth More spoke for everyone involved when he recorded: 'We all felt that this was something of which we could be proud.'[44] In 2000, Roy Ward Baker would say: 'It's my best film and my favourite film.'[45]

THE PRODUCER: WILLIAM MACQUITTY

The teaming of producer William MacQuitty, screenwriter Eric Ambler and director Roy Baker was particularly felicitous. All three had emerged from the wartime documentary movement into commercial feature film production and all three shared a commitment to values nurtured by that documentary movement: authenticity, emotional restraint, the idea of duty, concern with the predicament of ordinary people under stress. Film historians have perhaps underestimated the effect that the war had on the creative personnel of the film industry. Many of them saw active service, but even those who did not, lived through the terrors of the Blitz as they made films in or near London. Roy Baker wrote laconically of the bombs: 'They were a constant nuisance and sometimes frightening indeed. I do not wish to remind myself of any bomb stories.'[46] By the end of the war, they had learned of the unimaginable horrors of the Holocaust, of the Japanese prison camps and of the effects of the atomic bomb. It could not but have had an effect on their outlook.

It was not just that MacQuitty (*Above Us the Waves*, *The Black Tent*), Ambler (*The Cruel Sea*) and Roy Baker (*The One That Got Away*) all made films set in the war, it was more that their films often displayed a mood of bleak realism, a total absence of triumphalism and gung-ho heroics, and a stress on the realities of pressure, determination and duty.

The war and the immediate post-war period had seen documentarists such as Cavalcanti, Harry Watt, Pat Jackson and Jack Lee enter the world of feature film production, and established commercial directors such as Carol Reed, Thorold Dickinson and David MacDonald move into documentary-directing. The combination of visual authenticity and the realistic treatment of ordinary people characterizing their films became the hallmark of British cinema.

It all rubbed off on critical theory. As Robert Murphy has written: 'Realism as the dominant critical theory for the study of film seemed to grow out of the war, banishing impressionist, expressionist and surrealist experiments and the montage theories of Pudovkin and Eisenstein to the sidelines.'[47] The Italian neo-realist directors such as Rossellini and de Sica, who used real locations, non-actors and everyday stories, and the left-wing, social realist, location-shooting American directors such as Kazan, Dassin, Losey and Dmytryk also had a great influence on the dominant film aesthetic.

During the war MacQuitty had worked on the co-operative feature film about the Rochdale Pioneers, *Men of Rochdale* (1944), and had teamed up with the socialist filmmaker Jill Craigie to make the documentaries *Out of Chaos* (about war artists) and *The Way We Live* (on the rebuilding of blitzed Plymouth). As a producer MacQuitty had made his share of exotica. He had gone to Ceylon to film *The Beachcomber* (1954), a Somerset Maugham story about the rehabilitation of a drunken remittance man (Robert Newton) by a spinster missionary (Glynis Johns), and to Libya to make *The Black Tent* (1956), a Robin Maugham story about a doomed wartime romance between a British officer (Anthony Steel) and the daughter of an Arab sheikh (Anna Maria Sandri). But he was most closely associated with docu-dramas. He had produced *Blue Scar* (1948), Jill Craigie's drama about the effects of nationalization on the Welsh coal industry. He had teamed up with another woman filmmaker, Muriel Box, for *Street Corner* (1952), which dramatized the day-to-day work of policewomen in London. He had produced *Above Us the Waves* (1955), an austerely factual re-creation of the miniature submarine attack on the German battleship *Tirpitz*. The *Daily Worker* (7 April 1955) called the film 'a typically decent restrained British film' and the *Manchester Guardian* (2 April 1955), calling the film 'inspiringly authentic', took up a regular critical refrain when it said 'British war films are mostly better than those made in Hollywood because as a rule they keep to their main business – the tank battle, the convoy, the air raid. This film is, if anything, even more matter of fact than most of its kind.'

The fact that MacQuitty had worked on the co-operative feature film *Men of Rochdale*, that he produced a film advocating the nationalization of the coal mines (*Blue Scar*), that he made three films with the socialist writer-director Jill Craigie and that his first six films were directed by two women (Jill Craigie and Muriel Box) might suggest that MacQuitty was a left-wing filmmaker. He denies this: 'I have no political motivation of any description.' He was interested above all in the depiction of reality and insisted that this was his primary motivation. The desire for authenticity is what took him on location to South Wales, Ceylon and North Africa for his feature films and that inspired him to tell 'the true story' of the *Titanic*. His preference for women film directors over men was practical rather than ideological. He found them more reliable, responsible, cost-conscious and lacking in egotism than their male counterparts.[48]

A Night to Remember was to be MacQuitty's greatest cinematic achievement – and almost his last. Three days after the triumphant première of the film, he was informed that Rank would not be renewing his contract. He was to make only one further feature film (*The Informers*, 1963), but he moved first into television, setting up and running Ulster TV, and later developed a whole new career as a photographer and author, producing among others books on Abu Simbel, Tutankhamun and the Buddha.

THE DIRECTOR: ROY BAKER

Roy Baker had begun his film career in 1934 as a lowly production assistant or 'gofer' at the Islington studios of Gainsborough Pictures and worked on thirty-eight films over the next six years. It was seeing Robert Stevenson direct *Tudor Rose* (1936) that inspired him to become a director. His greatest influences in those early days were Carol Reed, for whom he worked on *Bank Holiday* (1937) and *A Girl Must Live* (1939), and who showed him how to handle actors and to get the best out of them, and Alfred Hitchcock, for whom he was second assistant on *The Lady Vanishes* (1938) and who taught him the necessity of pre-planning. Both these were to be key characteristics of Baker's own work. He joined the army on 15 February 1940 and after a year devoted to field exercises and constructing barbed-wire coastal defences he answered a call from the War Office for experienced filmmakers and spent the war making training films for the Army Kinematographic Service (AKS). At AKS he met Eric Ambler. They became friends and it was Ambler who gave Baker his first chance to direct a feature film after the war, *The October Man* (1947) which Ambler both wrote and produced. Baker subsequently directed Ambler's Cold War comedy thriller *Highly Dangerous* (1950).

His most significant early success was the submarine disaster film *Morning Departure* (1950), which led to Baker being immediately signed by 20th Century-Fox. In Britain he directed a Technicolor remake of *Berkeley Square* called *House on the Square* (1951) and in Hollywood three psychological thrillers (*Don't Bother to Knock*, *Night without Sleep* and *Inferno*). He was removed from the African adventure *White Witch Doctor* after shooting the location sequences in Africa and he found Hollywood unfulfilling artistically. The control of the studio system and its production methods was so tight that he felt the results were often formulaic pictures leaving little scope for directorial individuality. He returned to England to work for Rank and began with another successful sea picture, *Passage Home*. He turned down the chance to direct MacQuitty's production *Above Us the Waves*, because he had already directed a submarine picture and did not want to be known only as a director of sea stories. Later, he reflected in his autobiography: 'I should have decided to specialize in sea stories at that; there is plenty of variety in that field, and it is one of the things I'm good at.'[49] *A Night to Remember* would give him the chance to demonstrate that.

Baker was in no doubt about the importance of the director and the director's vision to the filmmaking process:

The director alone knows *completely* what the essentials are and how the performance and the technique at any one moment must fit into a scene, the scene into the sequence, and the sequence into the film, always with reference to the context of each moment – what came before and what is to come. All these decisions must be worked out in the director's mind before main photography starts, with the final details to be settled on the floor, during the shooting. Equally important the director alone knows what can be left out. The two OK words for the process are: selection and emphasis.[50]

Baker's absolute conviction of the director's centrality led him to ban dialogue directors from the set, to cut in the camera to prevent editorial tampering with his conception and to forbid actors to make private arrangements about their angles and lighting with cinematographers.

Roy Baker is one of the unsung *auteurs* of British cinema. As Sylvia Syms, who starred in his film *Flame in the Streets*, recalled: 'I had the greatest respect for the director Roy Baker. I've always considered him an underrated director. He was marvellous with that subject and I loved working with him. He was tough on the set but I thought he was very sensitive. All his films are entertaining, and he really had class.'[51]

Raymond Durgnat, one of the few film historians to analyse Baker's world-view, places him in the mainstream of British filmmaking. Dividing English filmmakers into moralists and romantics, he places Baker with the moralists (along with Thorold Dickinson, the Boulting Brothers, Peter Glenville and Joseph Losey) rather than the romantics (who include Michael Powell, David Lean and Terence Fisher). He wrote:

> The elements of doubt, disgust and despair which [Relph and Dearden] so rigorously exclude quietly but insistently infiltrate the films of Roy Baker, an *auteur* whose spiritual attitude, a kind of fair minded pessimism, precludes open revolt as it precludes acceptance. That stoic British acquiescence in arbitrary order reveals its secret roots in an existentialist scepticism which, settling for pragmatism, never, quite, discovers its full potential. His best films are in the class of Dickinson and Losey.

Linking Baker's *Tiger in the Smoke* to J. Lee Thompson's *Ice Cold in Alex*, Durgnat said:

> Such movies touch on self-criticism, a stress on life as basic frustration, deeper and older than Munich and Dunkirk. The characteristic mood of English movies is sombre, stoic, slightly depressed. Their complacencies

are those of relief rather than happiness, and, as such, more cynical and pessimistic, by implication, than at first appears. The mood seems almost independent of the particular story, and seems to arise not so much from the evolution of the plots ... but to precede it, or to be superimposed on it.[52]

It is interesting that much of this mood and outlook can be discerned in the great post-war films of Baker's mentor, Carol Reed: *Odd Man Out*, *The Fallen Idol*, *The Third Man* and *Outcast of the Islands*. It is hard not to relate this to the psychological effects of the Second World War on those who lived through it.

There is certainly no doubting the coherent artistic vision of Roy Baker in the 1950s. *The October Man*, his directorial debut, was written and produced by Eric Ambler for Filippo del Giudice's Two Cities Films. In his autobiography, Ambler dismissed it, saying 'it did nothing for Del's fortunes or for anyone else's'.[53] But it is one of the great ex-amples of British *film noir*, atmospherically lit, claustrophobically shot and psychologically intense. It is one of a post-war cycle of dramas about psychologically damaged men – *Mine Own Executioner* (1947), *The Small Back Room* (1948), *The Small Voice* (1948) – all of which reflected the contemporary concern about the effects of war on vulnerable males. John Mills, in many ways the archetypal Baker hero, plays an industrial chemist whose life has been wrecked by a bus crash which killed a little girl he was looking after. His head injuries and his guilt have made him suicidal. As he struggles to rebuild his life he becomes the prime suspect in the murder of a young woman who lodges at the same residential hotel as himself. Gossip by the hotel residents, repeated interrogations by the police, suspicion on the part of his workmates drives him to the edge. Aided only by a girl who loves him, he seeks to prove his innocence while at the same time battling the inner demons that are driving him back towards suicide. In the end, he unmasks the real murderer and holds on to his sanity. Mills gives a beautifully judged performance as a man desperately clinging to normality while his mind is in turmoil and driven to extreme measures to prove his innocence. The network of fear, desire, resentment, resignation and despair within the oppressive enclosed world of the shabby-genteel suburban hotel is acutely observed and shows Baker from the outset of his career fascinated by the predicament of the man trapped in an enclosed world. This will recur in the submarine of *Morning Departure* and ultimately in the doomed *Titanic* in *A Night to Remember*.

The legacy of the war lingers throughout his work. In *Tiger in the Smoke* (1956), the broken-down ex-servicemen reduced to crime, the psychopath who found the war a perfect arena for his violence, and the war widow seeking to come to terms with her loss and rebuild her life, are all casualties of the war. Raymond Durgnat called *Tiger in the Smoke* 'the most dreamlike English film since *Odd Man Out*', and it is for three-quarters of its length a superb thriller with metaphysical overtones, meditating on the nature of evil.[54] It is, however, flawed by the miscasting of Tony Wright as the evil Jack Havoc. Wright does not have the range or depth to suggest Havoc's complexity. Baker had wanted to cast Jack Hawkins or Stanley Baker in the role but had been overruled by Rank chief John Davis who insisted on Wright, whom he regarded, wrongly, as a rising star.

The film which most obviously prefigures *A Night to Remember* is *Morning Departure* (1950). Based on a stage play by Kenneth Woolard and adapted for the screen by former naval Lieutenant Commander William Fairchild, it was Baker's first maritime disaster film. It was probably inspired by the 1939 loss of the submarine *Thetis* in Liverpool Bay. In the film the submarine *Trojan* on peacetime manoeuvres strikes a mine and sinks. Only twelve of the sixty-five men survive. There are enough suits to allow only eight to escape. Four remain to wait for the submarine to be raised by a salvage team. The film focuses on the interplay of the four: the captain, Lieutenant Commander Peter Armstrong (John Mills), first officer Lieutenant Harry Manson (Nigel Patrick), stoker Snipe (Richard Attenborough) and ordinary seaman Higgins (James Hayter). Snipe, who endangers the survivors by panicking, recovers his courage and dignity by devotedly nursing Manson when he falls sick. Manson dies after a leak of chlorine gas. A storm causes the salvage operation to be abandoned and the three remaining submariners are doomed to die when their air runs out. The film ends with the captain leading them in reciting the naval prayer and the camera retreats from the submarine as the three prepare to die. The naval officer overseeing the salvage operation (Bernard Lee) concludes that they have been the victims of the traditional enemies of the seaman, bad luck and bad weather.

By an extraordinary coincidence the film was completed two months before the submarine *HMS Truculent* sank in the Thames estuary with the loss of sixty-four lives. What is more, parts of *Morning Departure* had been shot on the submarine *Tiptoe*, of the same class as *Truculent*. In those more sensitive and decent days when matters of good taste were still a consideration, this coincidence was seen not as a golden opportunity for promotional publicity but as a matter for anguished debate and heart-searching among producers, financiers and authorities about whether the film should be released at all. The Admiralty viewed it and gave it the go-ahead and the film censors stated: 'Had we found a false note in it we might have hesitated to pass it at such a time, but we think it deserves to be seen.' It was awarded an A certificate subject to the addition of a foreword to the film:

This film was completed before the loss of HMS Truculent. Careful consideration has been given to the desirability of showing it so soon after this grievous disaster. The producers feel, however, that the film will be accepted in the spirit in which it was intended, as a sincere tribute to brave men and as an expression of pride in the Royal Navy.[55]

The decision to release the film was vindicated. John Mills, describing the film as 'one of the films I am proud to have been associated with', recalled: 'I received many letters from relatives of the men who lost their lives; they all said, in so many words, that they were glad they had seen the film: it had made their loss bearable to see the gallant and courageous way in which men in the same situation as their loved ones faced almost certain death.'[56]

The style of the film (sober, restrained, semi-documentary), the theme (ordinary men dealing with an extraordinary crisis) and the ethos (stoical, resigned, dutiful) are quintessential Baker. The critical reception of *Morning Departure* reveals how much the film was in tune with the cultural sensibilities of that post-war decade, in which Britain was still recovering from the horrors of six years of war, there was still austerity and the atomic bomb and the Holocaust haunted the imagination. The critics were almost uniformly rapturous, praising everything about the film, with the terms 'superb', 'magnificent' and 'a triumph' repeatedly used.

It is fascinating that newspapers and magazines right across the political spectrum from the *Daily Mail* to the *Daily Worker* deployed the same terms of praise: in particular that the film was 'authentic' and that it was deeply and convincingly 'British' in its outlook and values. The two were frequently linked.

Dilys Powell in the *Sunday Times* (26 February 1950) said: 'Of all the films about submarines that I have seen ... *Morning Departure* seems to me the best: the most authentic, the most honourable, the most moving.' C. A. Lejeune in the *Observer* (26 February 1950) called it 'as honest a naval film as we have had since *In Which We Serve* and one of which everyone concerned can feel extremely proud'. The *Daily Express* (22 February 1950) said: 'The atmosphere of naval comradeship, of the humour and sympathy that are always present in disaster is superbly captured.' The *Daily Graphic* (24 February 50) noted that 'every line of dialogue rings true'. The *News of the World* (28 February 1950) thought it 'stirringly conveys the way brave men behave in the face of death' with 'just the right blend of diffidence and humour'. The *Daily Telegraph* (27 February 1950) observed: 'While we can make films like *Morning Departure* ... the British screen has a future. Here are fighting men seen as they are, without false heroics or sickly sentiment. I don't know when I have been more moved ... I have never seen a film of the sea that seemed ... more real ... or better acted.' *Reynolds News* (26 February 1950) declared: 'There is no attempt to depict melodramatic supermen, but a quietly penetrating study of simple, courageous, human beings' characterized by 'sympathy, comradeship and humour'. The *Manchester Guardian* (25 February 1950) called it 'a magnificent, and surely, genuine account of Royal Naval behaviour in the ultimate crisis'. The acting was generally very highly praised. John Mills in particular received tributes for the authenticity of his performance. The *Sunday Times* (26 February 1950) said Mills 'gives one of the subtly understated performances which had made his reputation. You can feel the tensions beneath the surface of the behaviour but the behaviour itself is controlled, businesslike and even.' The *Evening Standard* (23 February 1950) said: 'John Mills has never been better. It is impossible to believe he is anything but a lieutenant commander. He inspires as much confidence in his audience as in his men – a splendid performance.' *The Spectator* (19 February 1950) and *The Times* (24 February 1950) agreed.

The distinctive Britishness was recognized. The *Evening Standard* said: 'This is a magnificent picture. Not only is it a tribute to the navy but it revives in any doubting mind the true knowledge that there is no people on earth as dear and so wonderful as the British ... their courage is a triumph of understatement.' *The Spectator* said: 'The quietness, courage and humour of the British are characteristics which we recognize as being our dearest possessions, and this film is a glorious tribute to a country which still persists, in spite of provocation, in producing these virtues.' The *Daily Worker* said *Morning Departure* 'possesses those qualities which are particularly associated with the best British films, sincerity, humour, restraint and above all, integrity'. *The Star* said: 'No finer, more heartfelt picture has ever come out of a British studio than this restrained account of a peacetime submarine disaster.' *Reynolds News* declared: 'It displays some of the best qualities of British filmmaking, sincerity, understatement, complete authenticity of background and detail.'

Passage Home (1955), largely shot in the studio and demonstrating Baker's ability to handle a sea drama, culminated in a highly praised storm sequence. It also depicted a bleak and pessimistic universe. Peter Hutchings called it 'one of British cinema's most relentless portrayals of sexual repression'.[57]

The cattle boat *Bulinga*, returning to England from South America in the 1930s, has as captain 'Lucky' Ryland who is a martinet, an embittered first officer who believes he should be in command, a second officer who refuses to get involved and shuns responsibility, an ailing bosun and an intimidated youngster, Shorty, who is bullied. The crew are discontented because of the poor quality food supplied by the captain to cut costs. The arrival of an English governess Ruth Elton (Diane Cilento), stranded in South America and given passage home by the consul, causes tensions. Ryland (Peter Finch) wants to make the trip home in record time; the crew's discontent mounts as the bosun tries to keep the peace. Ryland is attracted to Ruth, proposes to her and when she refuses, tries to force himself on her. Second officer Vosper (Anthony Steel) intervenes to stop him with the news that the bosun has died. The captain gets drunk but manages with Ruth's help to get through the burial service. A terrific storm ensues. The captain pulls himself together, deploys his expertise and brings the ship through safely. Vosper saves Ruth from being swept overboard and commits himself to her. The previously bullied Shorty displays heroism by saving a fellow crewman from being crushed by the cattle.

The story is told in flashback, as Ryland, retiring from the company, is presented with a painting of the *Bulinga*, his first command. He will retire to a cottage on the coast still single and now without the career that has been his life. Vosper and Ruth, now married, attend and she watches Ryland leave for retirement with a tear in her eye. It is a film in which redemption is possible for some but not all. Vosper finds commitment and a wife; Shorty becomes a hero. The bosun, one of the decent characters who sought to protect Shorty from being bullied, falls ill and dies; the captain recovers his self-respect by handling the ship in the storm but is seen to have lived a lonely and loveless life.

Looked at as a whole, the films from the first part of Baker's career form a coherent oeuvre. 'Realism is my forte,' he said. His aim in film was 'to develop the documentary principle of realism to a higher degree'.[58] He returned again and again to the theme of ordinary people put into extraordinary situations, pushed to the edge and tested to the limit. How they cope is explored with extraordinary observation, sensitivity and insight. It is this preoccupation that links his psychological thrillers and his maritime dramas. Baker admitted in interview that this theme had 'always intrigued me, because most people lead comparatively ordinary lives and don't come up against enormous crises'.[59] It is the shaping theme of many of his most important works: with the trapped submariners facing death in *Morning Departure*; a psychologically damaged man being suspected of murder in *The October Man*; the captain and crew of the freighter in *Passage Home* coping with the tensions imposed by cutbacks, the presence of a woman on board and a phenomenal storm; the barrister hero of *Tiger in the Smoke* drawn into a shadowy underworld and facing the evil influence of a ruthless criminal to defend the woman he loves; Franz von Werra, the only German POW ever to escape from a British camp, fleeing across Britain and Canada in *The One That Got Away*; and the passengers and crew of *Titanic* facing disaster in *A Night to Remember*.

There is a strong vein of pessimism running through Baker's work, as Durgnat detected. Confronted with the description of himself as a 'a fair-minded pessimist', Baker today throws back his head and roars with laughter. But then he says: 'It's not something you know about yourself. I don't know how much you know about yourself.' He has always relied on instinct in choosing his film projects and there is certainly something which has drawn him to subjects with a tragic undertow.[60] The psychological legacy of the war may have something to do with it.

The unexpected outcome of *Morning Departure* (the deaths of the four submariners after the abandonment of the salvage operations), which contrasts with Hollywood where they would unquestionably have been rescued, again bespeaks pessimism. As do the lonely, unhappy life of 'Lucky' Ryland indicated by the flashback framework of *Passage Home*; the fact revealed in the final titles of *The One That Got Away* that, after all his travails and his successful return to Germany, Franz von Werra was shot down over the North Sea in 1941; and, of course, the fate of the *Titanic* in *A Night to Remember*.

Then there is the theme of quiet, determined, unselfconscious, middle-class professionalism. It can be seen in the actions and ethos of the professional seamen of *Morning Departure*, *Passage Home* and *A Night to Remember*. That pessimism, professionalism, and the theme of ordinary men in extraordinary circumstances also characterized films by

MacQuitty (*Above Us the Waves*) and Ambler (*The Cruel Sea, Yangtse Incident*). The capture of the submariners and the loss of one of the craft in *Above Us the Waves*; the loss of the *Compass Rose* in *The Cruel Sea*; and the losses sustained aboard the *Amethyst* in *Yangtse Incident* all give a downbeat feel to those docu-dramas.

Durgnat published his comments on Baker in 1970 and was reflecting essentially on Baker's films of the 1950s and early 1960s. But Baker underwent an extraordinary change of directorial identity, accompanied by an actual change of name. The first phase of his career ended in 1962 after a series of blows. Against his better judgement, he took on *The Singer Not the Song* (1960). He had several times refused the assignment stating: 'There was not one single element in this story that appealed to me. I was not interested in any way.' He wanted to do film versions of either the Willis Hall play *The Long and the Short and the Tall* or the Alan Sillitoe novel *Saturday Night and Sunday Morning*, which would both have been in his favoured realist mode. But John Davis and Earl St John of Rank rejected these properties and insisted on the Audrey Erskine Lindop novel *The Singer Not the Song*, which they envisaged as a vehicle for their contract star Dirk Bogarde. Rank tried and failed to secure a Hollywood co-star for Bogarde but in the end settled for John Mills. Bogarde had said: 'I promise you if Johnny plays the priest I will make life unbearable for everyone concerned.' Roy Baker recalled: 'He was as good as his word and he succeeded. There is nothing more to be said on that score.'[61]

The critics savaged the film. Baker recalled: 'They threw the book at the film and at me, wrecking a promising career. My self-confidence was severely dented, and it took me four years to get myself back on an even keel. I have never to this day fully regained the professional status I had at that time.' John Mills, interviewed in 1990, said of the film: 'That was one that went wrong. Dirk ... wasn't happy with the film, nor was Roy.' He believed Brando should have played the Bogarde role. Bogarde said: 'It was such a terrible script and they put John Mills in as the priest when it should have been someone like Paul Newman ... I did the whole thing for camp and nobody had any idea what was happening.'[62]

The casting suggestions of Mills and Bogarde for their co-stars give one of the clues to the film's failure. It needed to be done as a rip-roaring Hollywood melodrama. Instead, it is all too English and too under-powered. Mills plods along stolidly playing an Irish priest with an accent that comes and goes. Bogarde, clad in black leather, and alternately wielding a whip and stroking his cat, certainly does go for camp as the ruthless, manipulative atheist bandit Anacleto Comache. They are surrounded by a cast of British character actors, none of whom gives the slightest impression of being Mexican.

Despite its critical savaging in Britain, it became a success on the Continent where dubbing would have eliminated the English accents and where the dilemma of a Catholic priest loved by a beautiful girl chimed with the culture. It has also become a cult success with aficionados of camp, because of its strong homoerotic overtones. Even in 1961 Peter John Dyer found it 'strangely compelling', Bogarde 'a fetishist's dream' and the film 'as startling as a muffled scream from the subconscious'.[63] At the centre of the story, as the priest Father Keogh battles to save the soul of Anacleto and Anacleto schemes to destroy the priest's power over his village, a romantic triangle develops. Local beauty Locha and Anacleto both fall in love with the priest and both know they can never have him. In the end, Anacleto, shot down by the police, and the priest, shot by one of Anacleto's men, die with their arms around each other. Shot in Spain in lush Eastmancolor, it is far removed from Baker's 1950s films in mood and ethos. For it to have worked, it needed a Hollywood cast and a Hollywood director willing to imbue it with the psychological and sexual intensity and shameless melodramatic delirium of a *Duel in the Sun* or a *Johnny Guitar*. The emotional restraint and documentary authenticity that had characterized Baker's 1950s films made him temperamentally unsuited for the project. Baker's own verdict: 'I hated it. It broke my heart … it was a disaster. I should never have made it.'[64]

After *The Singer Not the Song*, Baker completed one further feature film, the powerful race-relations drama, *Flame in the Streets* (1961). Then in early 1961 Rank abandoned film production, giving as its reason falling cinema attendance and the rise of television. Baker regards this as a disaster for the British film industry. Apart from *The Singer Not the Song*, he had enjoyed his time at Rank and would have been happy to go on making films like *A Night to Remember* and *The One That Got Away*. Baker, who had always been at heart a company man, working successively for Two Cities Films, 20th Century-Fox, Rank and Hammer, was cast adrift, 'in the wilderness' as he puts it. He made a couple of independent features, *The Valiant* and *Two Left Feet*. The first he describes as 'a turkey' and the second, which he thought 'turned out well', was denied a proper release. He moved into television and from 1961 to 1967 directed many episodes of such popular series as *The Saint*, *The Avengers*, *The Baron* and *The Human Jungle*.

He did not return to films until 1967 with the Hammer production *Quatermass and the Pit*. At this point he changed his name. He had been getting mail and messages for a dubbing editor called Roy Baker, so he decided to call himself Roy Ward Baker, adopting his mother's maiden name as a middle name, to avoid confusion. The combination of the gap in his career, his name change and the total change of genre when he returned has resulted ever since in many people believing that Roy Baker and Roy Ward Baker are two different people. He laments it as 'a rash and damaging decision'. He still finds 'foreign critics who know me well as a Hammer director and are unaware of all the films I made prior to 1962'.[65] This misunderstanding is not perhaps surprising because from 1967 to 1980, in contrast to the social realism and black-and-white photography of his pre-1960 career, he worked almost exclusively in colour on horror films for Hammer and Amicus, films such as *The Vampire Lovers* (1970), *Scars of Dracula* (1970), *Doctor Jekyll and Sister Hyde* (1971), *And Now the Screaming Starts* (1972) and *The Monster Club* (1980). He brought to them his customary dedication and care and a concern to elicit the best from actors, as Ingrid Pitt attested in her autobiography.[66] He sought to bring realism and plausibility to the stories, but it is hard to resist the feeling that his heart was not in this genre as much as it had been in the social realism of his 1950s career. He remains proud of several of them (*Quatermass and the Pit*, *Asylum* and *Dr Jekyll and Sister Hyde*). Interviewed in 1976, he said: 'I'm not happy about being a "horror director". I did a few horror pictures … and I was automatically typed as a horror director which isn't right. I don't want to be and I don't like it.'[67]

Peter Hutchings, recognizing the critical neglect of Baker and trying to account for the extraordinary dichotomy in his career, sought an explanation in the structure and working conditions of the industry.[68] He argued that the medium-budget genre production in the 1950s was more fertile ground for the kind of personally authored work that Baker was producing than the world of series television and low-budget horror films that he entered in the 1960s. Certainly there could not be a greater contrast than that between Rank realism and Hammer horror and that reflects the dramatic changes in the nature of the British film industry.

THE WRITER: ERIC AMBLER

Eric Ambler, recruited at Baker's suggestion to write the script, was an accomplished writer of atmospheric espionage thrillers, several of which had been turned into notable Hollywood films (*The Mask of Dimitrios*, *Background to Danger*, *Journey into Fear*). During the war, working in the Army Kinematograph Service (AKS), he co-wrote Carol Reed's realistic drama of citizen soldiers, *The Way Ahead*. Ambler admitted that in the army he had 'lost the habit of a concentrated and solitary writing routine'.[69] So he turned his talents to scriptwriting for the collaborative medium of films.

For the most part he adapted existing books for the screen – among them H. G. Wells's *The Passionate Friends* (1948), Arnold Bennett's *The Card* (1952), H. E. Bates's *The Purple Plain* (1954) and Geoffrey Household's *Rough Shoot* (1953) – but he had also produced two original screenplays, *The October Man* (1947) and *Highly Dangerous* (1950), both of which had been directed by Roy Baker. Two of his most notable scripting achievements had been the maritime drama *The Cruel Sea* (from the novel by Nicholas Monsarrat) and *Yangtse Incident* (from the book by Lawrence Earl). Although they were different from the thrillers with which he had made his name, they and *A Night to Remember* share the characteristics identified by Gavin Lambert as typical of his work. Lambert wrote: 'Ambler has always written his stories like intelligence reports, the prose spare and lucid, the surface exact, even the atmosphere informational.'[70] These were the writing qualities he brought to his docudramas.

The Cruel Sea (1952) evoked the grim reality of the Battle of the Atlantic. Its epigraph ('The men are the heroes, the heroines are the ships, the only villain is the sea, the cruel sea') might equally have been applied to *A Night to Remember*. Covering the whole period of the war, it follows Captain Ericson and his officers on *Compass Rose* and later *Saltash Castle*. It charts the effects of the war on the officers both at sea – the threat from U-boats, storms, stress, exhaustion leading to nervous breakdown (Ferraby) and hardening (Ericson) – and at home: bereavement in the Blitz and marital infidelity. There are memorably grim scenes: the picking up of burned and oil-covered men from the sea at dead of night; Ericson having to plough through British seamen in the water to get to a lurking U-boat; the torpedoing of *Compass Rose*; and the cold, dark night of the survivors in the lifeboats. As in Baker's films, the themes are ordinary men being pushed to the limit, the nature and stresses of command, and the quiet, stoical performance of duty by meritocratic middle-class officers. Ericson is a professional seaman, a merchant ship captain before the war and his officers a barrister, a journalist and a bank clerk in civilian life. The one misfit is the former second-hand car salesman first officer who is a bully and a cad and ends up hospitalized with an ulcer.

The Cruel Sea garnered extravagant plaudits: 'the best film of the sea war to date' (*Time and Tide*, 4 April 1953), 'the finest film of war at sea ever made' (*Evening News*, 25 April 1953), 'the best British war film done in peacetime' (*Daily Herald*, 25 March 1953). When it came to specifics, it was the semi-documentary realism, the restraint and the Britishness that were singled out. The *News Chronicle* (27 March 1953) said: 'As a documentary the film is magnificent, and the action free from any false heroics.' The *Daily Mirror* (25 March 1953) called it 'a brilliantly, starkly factual war film' which 'does the nation proud and will impress the world ... it is harrowing, sometimes terrifying, yet all the time inspiring'. *The Times* (26 March 1953) pronounced it a 'remarkably good piece of honest, realistic cinema ... in the semi-documentary tradition which has gained so great a reputation for British films of war'. The *Evening Standard* (26 March 1953) said: 'The acting, direction and script come closer than any picture made since the war to a re-creation of fighting men in a fighting ship.' *The Times Educational Supplement* (10 April 1953) thought it 'recreates actuality, plunging its audience into the conviction that naval warfare really seemed like this at particular moments to an individual crew'. *The Spectator* (27 March 1953) noted that 'built on a foundation of understatement, the film, to a home audience at any rate, seems to concentrate on all that is fine and lovable in the national character. The brutal idiocy of war ... is presented with objective clarity and the strain imposed on the Royal Navy ... is stated baldly and without comment.' The *Manchester Guardian* (28 March 1953) pronounced it 'a noble, harrowing and at times distinctly tough tribute to bravery at sea'. The *Daily Worker* (28 March 1953) praised its 'careful, sober ... documentary style'. So all across the spectrum from left to right, from broadsheet to tabloid, there was consensus on its particular virtues and on what made a quality British film.

Ambler came to *A Night to Remember* fresh from scripting *Yangtse Incident*. This Cold War naval drama, filmed in 1956, re-created a famous episode of 1949 in which the frigate HMS *Amethyst*, sailing up the Yangtse River to deliver supplies to the British Embassy in Nanking during the civil war between the communist and nationalist forces, was fired on by the communist Chinese army, badly damaged and driven aground with heavy casualties (including the captain who died of his wounds). The assistant British naval attaché, Commander J. S. Kerans, was sent to take command and after weeks of cat-and-mouse negotiations with the communists, who insisted on a British apology and admission of responsibility, Kerans guided the *Amethyst* downriver in a dramatic escape which ended with the ship successfully rejoining the fleet.

The film's producer Herbert Wilcox wanted absolute authenticity and engaged Commander Kerans as technical adviser on the production. The First Sea Lord, Earl Mountbatten of Burma, promised full naval co-operation. Thanks to Mountbatten, Wilcox was able to obtain the actual HMS *Amethyst*, cocooned at Devonport and waiting to be broken up. It was taken to the River Orwell ('exactly like the Yangtse', according to Kerans) where the film was to be shot and much of the action was filmed aboard it. HMS *Essex* doubled for the ship on its escape, which had to be shot in a single take as the ship had been recalled for service at Suez. The film bore a foreword that explained that this was a true story shot aboard the *Amethyst* and apologized to those real-life participants, including the Chinese interpreter, who had to be omitted from the film because of the constraints of running time.[71]

Wilcox, clearly aiming to repeat the success of *The Dam Busters* (1955), engaged the director (Michael Anderson) and star (Richard Todd) of that film. Mountbatten, clearly recognizing a film about a heroic British naval exploit as positive propaganda for the navy, arranged for the première to be attended by Prince Philip and the Lords of the Admiralty. The opening and closing shots of the tattered white ensign flying defiantly, the closing message of congratulation from the king and the heroic Leighton Lucas score confer an upbeat air to the film, which *A Night to Remember* obviously lacks. But for much of its length the film's mood is restrained, sober and realistic.

Ambler based his script on Lawrence Earl's book but Wilcox recalls him saying to Kerans: 'We all know what happened. But what I'd like to know is what were your thoughts when you were deputed to do the job.'[72] This confirms the impression that one of Ambler's interests was the nature of command and the strains under which commanders operated. It is one of the continuing themes of both *The Cruel Sea* and *A Night to Remember*. In *Yangtse Incident* he focuses on Kerans's planning and execution of the escape.

A second aim is an authentic factual reconstruction of the actual event, and there are several parallels with *A Night to Remember*. The film begins by establishing the milieu of the ship with short scenes on the bridge, in the engine room, galley, stores and on deck. Then comes the attack, the desperate wireless messages for help and the failed attempt at rescue by another British ship, driven off by Chinese bombardment.

The evacuation of the wounded, the negotiations with the Chinese, the mechanics of the escape are all re-created with meticulous documentary accuracy. The long tracking shots along the lines of silent, wounded and exhausted crewmen testify to the toll the experience has taken on them.

The third theme of the film is the evocation of British character – stoicism, dedication to duty, laconic humour and understatement. These qualities are shared by all ranks of seamen: the injured Number One taking command after the captain is killed and keeping going on brandy and dry ginger; the single wireless operator transmitting continuously and uncomplainingly; the two captured and injured seamen refusing to acknowledge British guilt even at the risk of continuing as prisoners; Kerans, brisk and determined, masterminding the escape. This characterization too will be seen in *A Night to Remember*.

Yangtse Incident was received by the critics in very similar fashion to *The Cruel Sea*. The *Daily Mail* (2 April 1957) called it 'a magnificent tribute to a magnificent piece of naval heroism'; the *Daily Herald* (2 April 1957) thought it 'a great film ... perfectly cast'; the *Daily Sketch* (2 April 1957), 'a thundering good film'; *Reynolds News* (7 April 1957) 'a first-rate and inspiring film'; the *Daily Mirror* (5 April 1957) 'another triumph for Michael Anderson'.

On its style and content, the *Daily Mail* (2 April 1957) called it 'a film about real people who never lose their sense of humanity or their sense of humour'. *Reynolds News* (7 April 1957) thought it 'as lifelike as a newsreel. The bombardments are wonderfully realistic ... this realism is leavened with British Services' humour ... the heroism ... is understated.' *The News of the World* (7 April 1957) thought it 'meticulous ... there's no vainglory, no synthetic heroics'. *The Daily Worker* (6 April 1957), pointing out that it was told entirely from the British point of view, nevertheless found it 'brilliantly directed ... intensely moving ... because of its restraint and lack of flagwagging, it is a rattling good story'. *The Sunday Dispatch* (7 April 1957) said 'that this film is a duplication of what actually happened makes it so extraordinarily effective'. *The Financial Times* (29 April 1957) found it 'sober and painstaking ... directed ... with the traditional native film mixture of careful detail and emotional understatement'. *The Evening News* (4 April 1957) said: 'The admirable *Yangtse Incident* contents itself with the facts. And how intensely exciting and pride-filling these are.' *The Observer* (7 April 1957) said: '*Yangtse Incident* is directly in line with our best war documentaries, and shows at its strongest when it abjures decorative acting and concentrates on chaps who are used to playing chaps who don't expect to matter.' *The Sunday Express* (7 April 1957) called it 'a model of economic and vivid reportage'. The *Sunday Times* (7 April 1957) noted: 'Eric Ambler has stuck to the facts ... The playing of the crew is in keeping with the general reticence ... Michael Anderson has directed with decent respect: everything is modest, disciplined, unemphatic.' Here are all the virtues (factual, economic, understated, reticent) that the critics were to find in *A Night to Remember*.

In a published lecture Ambler reflected on the differences between novel-writing and scriptwriting. Recognizing that 'at its best film-making must be regarded as an art', he concluded that it was a 'complex discipline':

> It has been said that the problem of screenwriting is to say much in little, and then take half of that little out, and still preserve an effect of leisure and natural movement ... film is still primarily a visual medium ... screenwriting has very little to do with writing as a novelist understands the term. The only common denominators are a sense of story construction – and in this aspect the novel is closer to the film than the play – and the ability to create characters that breathe.[73]

These qualities of story construction and character drawing were to be invaluable when it came to turning Walter Lord's book into a filmscript.

Lord, a graduate of Princeton University and Yale Law School, had become fascinated with the story of the *Titanic* in 1926 when, as a small boy, he had crossed the Atlantic in her sister ship *Olympic*. He served in the American Intelligence Service in England during the Second World War. His training in assembling precise, detailed and accurate intelligence reports which he combined with a vivid writing style became the basis of a post-war writing career in which, while working in advertising, he researched and wrote accounts of great historical events – among them Pearl Harbor (*Day of Infamy*, 1957) and Dunkirk (*The Miracle of Dunkirk*, 1984). Over the years he had assembled accounts of the *Titanic* disaster, studied the official inquiry reports and interviewed sixty-three survivors. With this information, he pieced together an exact narrative, incident by incident, of the events of that fateful night. The result was *A Night to Remember*. Divided into ten chapters, each headed by a famous quotation associated with the tragedy, it opens with the lookout sighting the iceberg and then follows a mosaic of experiences, where people were, what they saw, how they reacted, even what they were wearing. The events unfold from 11.40 p.m. on 14 April when the *Titanic* struck the iceberg to 2.20 a.m. on 15 April, when it went down. Then comes an account of what happened in the lifeboats, the situation aboard the *Carpathia* racing to the rescue and the *Californian*, inexplicably standing off and ignoring *Titanic*'s rockets, and finally the arrival in New York of the survivors.

MacQuitty recalled that 'all three of us [i.e. Baker, Ambler and himself] got along very well'. They shared a commitment to telling the true story of the *Titanic*. In this they were part of a particular school of filmmaking that had grown up after the war, the 'now it can be told' school. While the war was on, propaganda constraints dictated what could be filmed. After the war, with these constraints relaxed, the true stories of the war began to be told, based not on official documents but on the memoirs of the people involved. During the war itself, there were no prisoner-of-war camp films but after the war the 'true stories' of *The Wooden Horse* (1950), *The Colditz Story* (1954) and *Albert R.N.* (1953) were filmed. During the war the details of undercover operations were obviously kept secret. After the war the 'true stories' of British secret agents in occupied Europe – *Odette* (1950), *Carve Her Name with Pride* (1958) – were filmed. The 'true stories' behind the famous operations to deceive the enemy – *The Man Who Never Was* (1956), *I Was Monty's Double* (1958) – were filmed. The 'truth' behind the great events of the war – *Dunkirk* (1958), *The Dam Busters* (1955) – was told. Real people were impersonated by actors; sometimes the people involved actually played themselves, or acted as technical advisers. The style was always sober, restrained, factual. The public, who had always had a healthy scepticism about propaganda, took to these films and made them box-office successes. In style and in approach, *Titanic* was one of them.

It is a commonplace that cinema cannot deal accurately with history. The dictates of the drama and the constraints of running time combine to ensure that the history in films is almost never authentic. Complex issues are simplified and individualized, events telescoped, significant figures omitted and confrontations invented to highlight themes. Most seriously, history is recast to emphasize present-day attitudes, approaches and preoccupations. The script for *A Night to Remember*, however, went to extraordinary lengths to achieve its desired authenticity. It had the advantage of concentrating largely on the last two hours of the *Titanic*'s life which fitted the film's running time exactly.

A film that prides itself in its authenticity nevertheless opens with an entirely fabricated sequence. A richly dressed lady, flanked by designer Thomas Andrews and White Star Line chairman J. Bruce Ismay, launches

Titanic with the traditional champagne bottle smashed against the hull and the blessing: 'I name this ship *Titanic*, may God bless her and all who sail in her.' This is followed by newsreel footage of a huge liner sliding down the slipway to the water. But this in fact never happened. The *Titanic* was launched without this ceremony and no footage of her launching survives, but the public will have imagined it happened and it makes an effective opening. The newsreel seems to be a combination of the launching of the *Queen Elizabeth* in 1938 and of the *Mauretania* in 1939. According to *Titanic* experts Don Lynch and Ken Marschall, speaking in their DVD commentary, there is no actual footage of *Titanic* in the film. Such archive footage as can be identified is of *Lusitania* or *Aquitania*.

However, much of the dialogue in the film is produced verbatim from Lord's book and thus from the memories of survivors. The scenes aboard the *Carpathia* and the *Californian* are exactly as participants recalled them. The scenes in the wireless room of *Titanic* are also re-created precisely, as recalled by survivor Harold Bride. Time and again, Lord's reported exchanges are reproduced in the film; Arthur Ryerson insisting that his son is only thirteen and must be allowed in a boat; Miss Evans telling Mrs Brown, 'You go first. You have children waiting at home'; an hysterical fat woman protesting, 'Don't put me in the boat. I don't want to go in the boat. I've never been in a boat in my life'; the honeymooners agreeing, 'We started together. We'll finish together'; Mrs Straus insisting on staying behind with her husband.

In the interests of dramatic coherence, several of the characters are composites, their words and actions drawn from several different real-life figures, a practice Lord approved in the interests of clarity.[74] Hoyle, the gambler who gets into the lifeboat on the starboard side, is a composite of several such figures, men determined to save themselves at all costs. Murphy, who leads the steerage girls to the lifeboat, is a composite of several Irish emigrants. Mr and Mrs Robert Lucas are composites of several married couples, notably Mr and Mrs Lucien Smith and Mr and Mrs Arthur Ryerson. The speeches they made to each other are given to the Lucases. The honeymooners, Mr and Mrs Clarke, are composites of several honeymoon couples. Rank were concerned about the possibility of libel suits, and counsel's opinion was sought from Helenus Milmo QC. On his advice J. Bruce Ismay, who had previously only appeared in the Nazi *Titanic*, is referred to throughout only as 'The Chairman', and Sir Cosmo and Lady Duff Gordon became Sir Richard and his wife Lady Richard.

Although there is not a single star role per se, Second Officer Lightoller becomes the leading person among the officers. Actions by other officers, the firing of shots and the bawling out of Ismay, for instance, are attributed to Lightoller. Lightoller's decisive action in taking charge of the upturned boat and keeping it on an even keel figures prominently in the lifeboat sequence. The other officers are much less prominent.

The film, like previous versions, depicts the *Titanic* in its final plunge standing upright in the water and sliding down into the water intact. This is how the end was reported by such authoritative commentators as Lawrence Beesley, C. H. Lightoller and Colonel Archibald Gracie, confirmed by the US Senate Inquiry and depicted in contemporary illustrations. But even at the time, other survivors such as Jack Thayer reported the ship breaking in two before the plunge. This interpretation was confirmed when the wreck was located and found to be in two parts. James Cameron's *Titanic* (1997) duly depicted the ship breaking in two.

For all these alterations and compressions, the film is regarded by *Titanic* buffs, with their encyclopaedic knowledge and their hawk-eyed attention to detail, as by far the most factually accurate cinematic account – as the definitive *Titanic* film.

THREE
A Critical Analysis
of the Film

THE VISUAL STYLE

Interviewed in 1961, Roy Baker made it clear that his priorities lay with the actors and the script:

There is a good deal of talk about the technical aspect of film making. Technique, surely, is A B C – something to be mastered, then forgotten and then deliberately abused. Of course one has to be very careful to be sure that you do know technique well enough to start to abuse it ... From the point of view of somebody who thinks he knows his technique, I feel that I can devote myself to working with the actors without worrying about technique. The actor is the mode of expression, and the other important factor is of course the writer. What you are trying to do is to tell a story to an audience through a medium of actors, because they are the only contact that you have between yourself and the audience. Anything that you can do to make them more effective must be to the ultimate good of telling a story, and arousing an emotional response from the audience ... I think automatically you derive from the script a sense of the shape of a scene, and you will begin to see where the emphasis lies ... I try to get the script to be as perfect as possible before I start production on a picture. I pry over every line of dialogue, every comma. I've been known to reprint a page just because a comma was wrong. I've had so much experience of people getting the wrong impression from scripts. As far as my principal players are concerned, I always try to have at least a couple of hours quietly with each one before I start production, going through their whole part and seeing the story from *their* point of view. This can be very interesting because you re-tell the whole story as seen from that particular point of view and not from either my point of view or the audience's. This preparation exposes all sorts of rough spots, which have to be papered over.[1]

Roy Baker outlined his regular mode of directing in his autobiography:

> My method was, and still is, to present – with the actors – a complete mechanical layout of each scene as it came along, so as to enable the crew to get to work. Everyone then knows what the requirements are going to be. Once the crew have finished their arrangements I take the actors through two or three rehearsals, during which all the minor details are ironed out and the final polish is applied and the actors are led naturally into the first take. This is the tried and tested procedure used by almost every director in the world. But as soon as the crew start to set up, anybody can barge in with comments and suggestions, mostly concerning minor points which will anyway be dealt with at a later stage.[2]

Roy Baker's particular strengths (his belief in pre-planning and handling of actors) were well suited to this project. Since, like most films, *A Night to Remember* was not shot in sequence (only two of Baker's films, *Don't Bother to Knock* and *The Anniversary*, were), effective continuity was crucial, particularly with the decks being lifted to a different angle hydraulically depending on which scene was being shot. The direction of the actors was also vital, as any false note must be avoided in what was intended to be a realistic re-creation. The result of Baker's concern for the acting is that this is a film in which all the members of the very large cast emerge as rounded, three-dimensional, thought-through characters. The film is so moving precisely because there are so many people about whom we, the audience, care.

From the outset, Baker's directorial style had been described by critics as 'unobtrusive', 'unpretentious' and 'restrained', descriptions he is happy to accept, since he did not wish the audience to be camera-conscious. He worked out his set-ups and angles by instinct. He describes himself as an 'instinctive director. You should always follow your instinct – for good or for ill.' On *A Night to Remember* he adopted the style of sober realism familiar from his previous films. The script was constructed like a jigsaw, a mosaic of short scenes, and it was essential to avoid visual flashiness that might distract the audience from following the story and the large cast of characters. His shooting style was then a classic one of medium- and long-shots for action and exposition with close-ups for dramatic emphasis.

This was a film in which close-ups were sparingly used, however, as if to emphasize the collective rather than the individual nature of the experience. There are intercut close-ups of Murphy and an immigrant girl, establishing their attraction to each other. There is a dramatic close-up of Murdoch watching the ship approaching the iceberg. There are close-ups of the captain realizing the enormity of the disaster, ordering everyone to 'abandon ship', listening to 'Nearer, My God, to Thee', looking out at the *Californian* and saying, 'God Help You'. Finally, there is a close-up of his face before he retreats to the bridge to die. There are close-ups of Captain Rostron realizing the *Carpathia* won't arrive in time and later seeing the first lifeboat. There are intercut close-ups of Andrews and Lucas as Andrews advises him to evacuate his family. There are close-ups of Murdoch looking disgusted as Ismay enters a lifeboat, of the faces of people in the boats hearing 'Nearer, My God, to Thee' and Ismay in the lifeboat looking appalled as the ship goes down. There is a close-up of an unknown woman clutching her baby in the lifeboat as the ship goes down. There are intercut close-ups of Lightoller and Gracie discussing the reasons for the disaster. Baker's camera movements are designed to be unobtrusive, and for the most part he tracks on movement: reverse tracking ahead of people walking down ship's corridors, parallel tracking as they enter the dining room or walk on the deck.

Baker regularly uses dolly-shots to capture the reactions of characters to the events, and also uses dolly-shots to draw the audience's attention wordlessly to some of the causes of the tragedy. He dollies in three times to an ice warning which has been spiked and ignored and into the earphones of the sleeping wireless operator on the *Californian* through which the SOS is coming from the *Titanic* unheard. Dolly-shots continually underline the irony of the situation. There is a dolly into an abandoned jewel case after Edith Russell returns to her cabin for her lucky pig. The camera also dollies in to Andrews gazing up at the painting in the smoke room. It is 'The Approach to the New World', an approach the *Titanic* will never see.

One of the most important elements in the film is the intercutting. The formal structure is provided by the intercutting between the mounting disaster on the *Titanic* and the complacent reactions aboard the *Californian*, between the *Carpathia* steaming to the rescue and the *Titanic* sinking, between the scenes in the first- and third-class areas, on the bridge, in the wireless room and the engine room. The pace of the cutting increases as the disaster moves towards its climax.

Fascinatingly, *A Night to Remember* conforms to many elements in the code of conduct for documentaries laid down by Cavalcanti, himself a documentarist turned feature-filmmaker, in 1948. Cavalcanti preferred the term 'neo-realist' to 'documentary' which he felt 'has a taste of dust and boredom'. The maxims that Baker realizes in his film are:

5. Do not forget, when you are filming, each take is part of a sequence and each sequence is part of the whole: the most beautiful take, taken out of place, is worse than the most banal.

6. Do not invent camera angles when they are not necessary: gratuitous angles are distracting, and destroy emotion.

7. Do not overuse rapid 'montage': an accelerated rhythm can be just as monotonous as the more pompous wide shot.

8. Do not make excessive use of music: if you do the audience will no longer hear it.

9. Do not overcharge your film with synchronised sound effects: sound is never better than when used suggestively.

10. Do not order too many special effects, nor make them complicated.

11. Do not film too many 'close ups' ... In a balanced film they will come naturally: when there are too many, they tend to suffocate each other, and lose their significance.

12. Do not hesitate to deal with human elements and human relationships.

13. Do not be confused in your argument: a truthful subject should be told with clarity and simplicity.[3]

The result is a film that can be justly described as a neo-realist classic.

THE NARRATIVE

The *Titanic* is launched by a richly dressed lady. Then the credits unfold in alphabetical order over shots of the sea (in mute reproach to the *Titanic* memorial in Belfast) and William Alwyn's surging title music with its threatening drumbeats. A title identifies the year 1912. After a shot of a vintage train, a young couple in a carriage are joking about an advertisement for Vinolia Otto luxury soap for the use of first-class passengers on the *Titanic*. 'The rest don't wash, of course,' says the young man with a smile. This ironic comment hints at the evocation of the class structure which the film will embody. The actual advert is reproduced in the illustrated edition of Lord's book. Another passenger, symbolically named Mr Bull (i.e. John Bull, the typical Englishman), provoked by the comment, objects to the insulting of the ship. The young woman reveals that her husband Charles Herbert 'Bertie' Lightoller is the second officer on the *Titanic*. The passenger is mollified and declares the ship 'unsinkable' and 'the symbol of man's final victory over nature and the elements'. This sets up the *hubris* which is represented by the claim repeated throughout the film that the ship is 'unsinkable'. It will be met by *nemesis* and will have its counterpart in Lightoller's final remarks about never being certain about anything again. The scene also establishes Lightoller as a leading character in the film, imbued with the familiar sturdy, decent, good-natured Kenneth More persona.

In the White Star Line offices, the scale of the operation is conveyed by the reading out of lists of provisions and of the numbers of passengers in each class, 2,208 in all. Three successive scenes record the departure of an upper-class couple (Sir Richard and his wife), a middle-class couple (the honeymooning Clarkes) and an Irish emigrant party due to travel steerage. This sets up the class structure of the ship.

Lightoller and his wife discuss his role as second officer of *Titanic* and the possibilities of promotion, and his plan to buy her frilly garters as a present in new York. Their affectionate banter and parting kiss establish them as a loving couple and reinforces the role of Lightoller as a leading figure. He is the only one of the officers whose private life is glimpsed.

April 10 flashes up; passengers board the *Titanic*. On the bridge, Captain Smith and his officers, the chairman (Ismay) and the designer of the ship Thomas Andrews discuss the sailing and it is made clear that there will be no attempt on the record, refuting the oft-repeated legend that Ismay ordered captain Smith to proceed at full speed. The ship sails in original newsreel footage of an unidentified ship.

April 14 flashes up with a snatch of Alwyn's music, and the final day begins. From now on in this section of the film, there is intercutting between the *Californian* and the *Titanic*, highlighting one historical theme of the night (the failure of the *Californian* to come to the *Titanic*'s aid), and there is intercutting between different parts of the ship, establishing the milieu, in a similar manner to Ambler's *Yangtse Incident* script. At the captain's table on *Titanic*, Ismay explains to the other guests that the ship is 'steady as a rock'. Everyone is in good spirits. On the *Californian*, Captain Lord is drinking tea on the bridge. He receives ice warnings and goes down from the bridge to his cabin, ordering the warnings to be sent on.

Titanic wireless operator Bride brings ice warnings to the first-class dining room and they are taken by a steward to the captain, who tells Ismay and the others about them but promises to keep a good watch. On the *Californian*, Wireless Officer Evans listens in to *Titanic*'s constant stream of personal messages. Captain Lord spots ice floes and orders all other ships to be informed.

In steerage, emigrant passengers celebrate. Murphy leads the singing of 'I'm Off to Philadelphia in the Morning' and then they dance an Irish jig. Sir Richard and his wife go into dinner in first-class, and American millionairess Molly Brown regales a British gentleman with the story of her life. Cut to the engine rooms where Thomas Andrews is inspecting the furnaces and talking to the stokers. Cut to the wireless room where John Phillips relieves Harold Bride and sends a stream of messages. Phillips spikes the ice message and continues to send personal messages.

Lightoller gives orders on the bridge. The Clarkes stroll on the deck. Sir Richard and his lady take their seats in the lounge as the band play 'The Blue Danube'. Captain Smith on the bridge orders that the lookouts should keep eyes open for ice. Lightoller relays his orders. The *Californian* spots an ice field and stops. Captain Lord orders other ships warned. The lookouts receive their orders to watch for ice. Lightoller hands over to Murdoch on the bridge and does his rounds. First-class passengers who are betting on the ship's speed ask him for information which he smilingly declines to give. A lady passenger, gazing admiringly at Lightoller, presses him to accept a drink which he politely declines.

Lightoller recognizes one of the gamblers, Jay Yates, in the saloon as a professional. He asks a steward to keep an eye on Yates. The *Californian* wireless operator tries to contact the *Titanic* and is ordered to keep out and not interrupt the dispatch of personal messages. The *Californian* wireless officer turns in for the night. Lightoller encounters the ship's doctor, Dr O'Loughlin, who is calling on Andrews with a nightcap to encourage him to break from working obsessively, checking on everything.

The build-up to the crash is now signalled by intercutting between characters: the engineers in the engine rooms, baker Charles Joughin baking bread, Lightoller turning in for the night, the gamblers still gambling, the stewards clearing the dining room. The *Californian* sights the *Titanic* and Lord orders her to be signalled with a Morse lamp. There is a dolly in to Ismay's face as he sleeps; in the first-class corridor a man slips out of his cabin, raps on the door of a cabin opposite, a woman's hand emerges and leads him in, epitomizing the classic amorous assignation of the aristocratic country house weekend. The Lucas children are put to bed by their mother and the camera tracks in to their rocking horse (which will reappear later among the debris from the ship).

The iceberg is sighted by the lookouts and the bridge informed. We do not see the iceberg at this stage or the berg slicing into the side of the ship, as we did in the 1929 *Atlantic* and the 1953 *Titanic*. Instead, there is a flurry of rapid intercutting: bells ringing, lights flashing, watertight doors closing, the iceberg looms, close-ups of Murdoch's horrified face. There is a perceptible shudder in the dining room. Ice cascades down on to the deck from the berg. Water pours into the engine room through the gash in the plates and men hurl themselves out under watertight doors.

Captain Smith comes to the bridge and sends for Andrews, who will assess the damage. Stewards and engineers discuss possible reasons for the sudden stop. An exhilarated young man dashes into the first-class saloon with a great chunk of ice. Steerage passengers kick it about on deck in an impromptu game of football. Ismay blusters and demands that they get underway, bewildered by news of the damage. This establishes the contrast between the unconcern of the passengers and the seriousness of the situation obvious on the bridge.

The steam is let off in a deafening roar. Lightoller, roused by the steam, gets up. The furnaces are raked and put out to prevent explosions. Andrews inspects the damage. Passengers get up to inquire why they have stopped. 'There's talk of an iceberg ... ' says a steward to one passenger. Wireless operator Bride gets up and joins Phillips. Andrews demonstrates to the captain the certainty that the ship will sink in an hour and a half or two hours. 'She can't sink, she's unsinkable,' says Smith. The claim that she is unsinkable is repeated by various characters as the disaster unfolds. Captain Smith gives orders to prepare to evacuate the ship. There must be no panic. But there are 2,200 passengers on board and room in the lifeboats for only 1,200.

The captain summons his officers and issues orders. Ismay cannot believe what is happening. Lightoller orders the lifeboats swung out. The wireless operators are instructed to send the distress signal, CQD. Bride suggests that Phillips use the new signal, SOS. On the *Californian* the wireless operator is asleep and does not receive the message. Stewards rouse the guests. One steward argues with a passenger who can't speak English. Foreigners see water coming into their cabins and hasten to get out. Another steward has things thrown at him when he tries to rouse sleeping crew members: 'Hooligans,' he snorts. Ismay interferes as Lightoller is trying to get the lifeboats out and is ordered away. Stewardess Mary Sloan is asked by Andrews to put her lifejacket on, to encourage the passengers to do likewise. An upper-class woman protests, 'Everyone knows this ship can't sink.' Cut to water pouring into engineering. Steerage passengers put on their lifejackets.

On the bridge of the *Carpathia* the third officer and the wireless operator, Cottam, joke about the former's amorous exploits. Cottam, about to turn in, receives the SOS from *Titanic* and, when the officers on the bridge refuse to believe him, he rouses the captain. Captain Rostron gets up, orders the ship turned round and headed for *Titanic* and makes arrangements to receive survivors. It will take four hours to reach *Titanic*.

Back on the *Titanic* lifeboats are lowered. Bride reports to the captain that the *Carpathia* is on its way but the *Californian* is not replying. The captain orders distress rockets fired, and the women and children into the lifeboats. The *Californian* sees the rockets but does nothing about it. Women and children only are allowed in the boats on the port side; but women and children first on starboard. The first-class passengers gather on deck but some object to entering the boats. One first-class man insists the women will be safer on board than in the boats. Wallace Hartley and the band play ragtime to calm their fears. The gamblers continue to play cards, saying that the ship cannot sink. Pumping keeps the ship afloat for a time. Andrews tells a steward to collect and distribute spare blankets and lifejackets.

Lucas asks Andrews for advice and is told the ship is doomed and he should get his family into the boats. The bulkhead in the furnace room goes and the stokers evacuate. Champagne is served to first-class passengers. On deck, the children are excited by the sight of the distress rockets. A first-class passenger refuses to put on her lifejacket. Molly Brown encourages reluctant first-class passengers to enter the boats. Gates from steerage into first-class are kept locked and steerage passengers are not allowed through. The engineers are asked to keep the engines going as long as possible to maintain power for lights and the wireless.

On *Carpathia*, Captain Rostron issues further orders. Baker Charles Joughin gives up his seat in a lifeboat to allow a mother to join her child. Ismay, continually interfering, is ordered away by Lightoller. Boats are lowered. Fourth Officer Boxhall supervises the sending up of the rockets, puzzled at the failure of the *Californian* to react. On the *Californian*, Captain Lord is alerted to the rockets by his first officer and orders him to signal with a Morse lamp; but it cannot be seen from the *Titanic*. Joughin retreats to his cabin to drink whisky. Protesting first-class passengers are ordered into the boats by Andrews.

The steerage passengers are still being held below, but steerage passenger Murphy finds a way up to the deck for his party and gets the women into the boats. Rockets continue to be fired. A hysterical fat woman objects to being put in a lifeboat. Lucas puts his family into a lifeboat and steps back. Hartley and the band move out on deck, still playing. Lightoller orders men out of the lifeboats. Edith Russell goes back for her lucky pig and then enters a lifeboat. Major Arthur Peuchen puts on his lucky pin. The card-players continue playing but the increasingly nervous Hoyle leaves to look for a boat. Joughin continues to drink. Phillips continues transmitting but can raise no ship closer than *Carpathia*. The captain orders Quartermaster Rowe to signal the *Californian* with a Morse lamp. The steerage passengers are getting restless, so the captain orders guns to be distributed among his officers. A hysterical woman passenger refuses to be parted from her husband. The Clarkes decide to stay on board together.

Molly Brown, realizing that her boat has only one seaman in it, requests another and Lightoller allows Major Peuchen, a yachtsman, to shin down a rope and help with the rowing of the lifeboat. Joughin is still drinking. Steerage passengers become increasingly restless. Mrs Straus refuses to leave Mr Straus and this confirms the Clarkes in their decision. Lightoller allows the thirteen-year-old son of Arthur Ryerson into a boat.

Sir Richard and his wife talk about men being allowed in the boats on the starboard side. Hoyle overhears them and goes to the starboard side. The ship's boys waiting for orders are reprimanded for smoking. Lightoller removes men from the lifeboat. Guggenheim objects to his lifejacket and sends for his valet. The Richards and Hoyle are admitted to a lifeboat by First Officer Murdoch. Locked gates are broken down by steerage passengers with an axe. Guns are issued. Pumping is abandoned.

Stokers man a half-empty lifeboat. Women and children from steerage are allowed on to deck but find the lifeboats gone. Joughin finds water barring his way out. In the smoking room, Yates writes a note. The Clarkes sit together and W. T. Stead calmly reads. The rockets have all gone – there is no response from the *Californian*. The captain looks across at the *Californian*, murmuring, 'God help you'. Ismay assists with the evacuation. Yates gives a lady passenger the note to send to his sister. Another gambler remarks: 'I've never been a good loser. I intend to get into a boat.' Panic sets in. Ismay gets into a boat.

The captain visits the wireless room. There is no further news. He asks Phillips to tell the *Carpathia* to hurry. Cottam receives the news on *Carpathia* and takes it to the captain. On *Titanic* panic mounts. Lightoller, trying to keep order, has to fire shots in the air. Molly Brown in a lifeboat gives her shawl to a shivering woman and organizes the ladies to row. Miss Evans gives way to a married woman to occupy the last place in the last lifeboat. In the smoking room, Guggenheim and his valet appear in full evening dress; Yates plays solitaire; Stead reads his book; Andrews looks at his watch. The collapsible boat is being unlashed by Lightoller and crew. Andrews advises the Clarkes on how to escape the sinking ship. The engines fail and the engineers are ordered out. The captain releases Phillips and Bride, but Phillips continues to transmit. A stoker steals Phillips's lifebelt, is stopped by Bride, and knocked out by Phillips. The captain orders, 'Abandon ship'. People flee to the stern, some leap into the water. Hartley and his men play 'Nearer, My God, to Thee'; the cellist sings. The captain listens to it and then goes back on to the bridge to face the end. The collapsible is floated off. Lightoller and Colonel Gracie in the water head for it. Andrews is alone in the smoking room. He declines to escape, accepting death as the price of his design failures. Joughin throws chairs into the water to act as a raft. As the ship tilts, bread tips out of racks, plates fall on to the floor. The rocking horse and chairs slide across the floor. An engineer is crushed by moving machinery. The lights go out. A steward takes hold of a lost child. The people still on board retreat to the stern. The ship goes down. The Clarkes, struggling in the water, are killed by a falling funnel. The people at the stern recite the Lord's Prayer in many different languages and the ship goes under. Molly Brown wants to row back for survivors, but Quartermaster Hitchens refuses, saying the boat will be swamped. Survivors struggle in the water.

Fifth Officer Lowe's boat returns for survivors; Sir Richard's boat does not return. Daniel Buckley is discovered in one of the boats in women's clothes. The watch on the *Californian* notes that the steamer has disappeared. Yates, denied access to the upturned boat, swims away; Lightoller urges him, in vain, to come back. Lightoller takes command of the upturned boat. Murphy and Gallagher are taken on board. Joughin holds on to the side and is eventually taken aboard. Lightoller keeps the boat trim. An upper-class woman complains about a man smoking in one of the boats. Women call for husband and child and complain about the cold. Edith Russell's musical pig cheers up a child. The *Carpathia*'s rockets are sighted. The lifeboats signal to the *Carpathia*. Lightoller and Gracie discuss the disaster. They agree there are a lot of ifs:

LIGHTOLLER: If we'd been going slower. If we'd sighted the iceberg
a minute earlier. If there'd been enough lifeboats.
GRACIE: You're not God.
LIGHTOLLER: No seaman ever thinks he is. But we were so sure. Even
though it's happened – it's still unbelievable. I don't think I'll ever feel
sure again – about anything.

The *Carpathia* takes the survivors on board. A memorial service is
held on board *Carpathia*. The camera tracks from the clergyman through
the survivors: Peuchen, Bride, Mrs Lucas, Molly Brown, Hoyle, the
Irish group, Edith Russell, Gracie. Captain Rostron sends for Lightoller
to see the site of the disaster. A message arrives from the *Californian*
offering help. 'All that was humanly possible has been done,' says Rostron. Debris floats by, including a cello and the Lucas rocking horse.
The end titles announce that the disaster led to changes. After it there
would be enough lifeboats for all, unceasing radio vigil and Atlantic ice
patrols.

CLASS

The importance of the theme of class is established at the outset by three
successive scenes. One after another we see representatives of each of the
three classes setting out for the *Titanic*. The aristocrat Sir Richard and
his wife leave their stately home and depart by carriage for the ship. Their
luggage is enumerated by the servants and a group of workhouse children
lined up outside cheer them as they leave. 'Show Sir Richard and his lady
wife how much we respect them,' says their teacher. 'The workhouse
children making sure of their Christmas turkey from the home farm,'
comments one of the servants cynically. Immediately after this, we see
a middle-class honeymoon couple, the Clarkes, leaving by car, seen off
by friends and relatives from a suburban home. Finally, in Ireland, a
group of Irish emigrants who will be travelling steerage are seen off in
a pony and trap by their neighbours and the parish priest. They include
the historically authentic Farrells, Martin Gallagher, Kate (either Gilnagh,
Murphy or Mullins, all travelling together) and the composite 'Murphy'.
These representatives of the three classes will be continuing figures
through the story whose unfolding fates we will follow.

According to Roy Baker, the first draft of the script did not contain
the steerage passengers and he insisted that they be included. MacQuitty
and Ambler initially thought that they would encounter problems from

3. *The upper class: the captain's table.*

4. *The lower class: the emigrants in steerage.*

5. *The middle class:
the honeymooning
Clarkes (Ronald
Allen and
Jill Dixon).*

3–5. *Class: the film reflected the strict class hierarchy of Edwardian
England by intercutting the experiences of the three classes.*

Rank if they did. But eventually all agreed that the steerage passengers
should be included and there was no objection from Rank. So is the film
intended as a critique of the class system? Roy Baker says it is not:

> We had no political agenda. All three of us saw it in the same way – as
> a chance to do something authentic. It was not a critique, it was a
> demonstration of class attitudes that everyone accepted at that time. The
> real meaning is that here was a world that was about to be overturned.
> You don't have to hit people over the head to demonstrate this. What I
> tried to demonstrate was that these class attitudes were accepted by the
> whole population from top to bottom. It was never an attempt to critique.

MacQuitty agrees. His aim, too, was 'reality'.[4]

Class, though, is one of the structuring features of the film as it cuts
back and forth principally between first class and steerage but also to
second class. In steerage, the emigrants sing 'We're Off to Philadelphia

in the Morning' and Murphy exchanges glances with a shy emigrant as a jig is struck up and the dancing ensues. Baker cuts from this to long elegant tracking shots as Sir Richard and his lady move urbanely through the first-class dining room to their table. The differences of lifestyle and ethos are thus effectively established.

Thereafter class recurs throughout. As the second-class Clarkes stroll on the deck, Mrs Clarke warns, 'This is first class,' and her husband jokingly replies, 'They're welcome to it on a night like this,' and they retreat to their own class. In second class, three drunken steerage passengers encounter a steward and say they are looking for their bunks. He tells them that they have strayed into second class. 'No offence, lad,' says the leading intruder, and they obediently retreat to steerage.

After the ship has struck the iceberg and the steerage passengers have an impromptu game of football with the chunks of ice on the deck, a first-class passenger remarks to his female companion, 'Let's go down and join the fun,' only to be told, 'But they're steerage passengers.' As the stewards circulate to rouse the passengers to put on their lifejackets and proceed to the lifeboats, the first-class passengers are roused respectfully and tactfully and the third-class passengers are ordered up peremptorily.

As the evacuation into lifeboats begins, first-class passengers complain volubly. 'It's too tiresome of them – everybody knows this ship can't sink,' says one. Others complain about the inconvenience and champagne is served to them as they sit in their lifejackets. Andrews and Lightoller have to start ordering women into the boats, overriding their protests. Other first-class passengers mob the purser's office, seeking to retrieve their jewels.

As the crisis mounts, the class divisions begin to break down. While the steerage passengers are held below, the Irish group whose fortunes we have followed since the beginning decide to make their own way up to the lifeboats. Murphy finds a way. He leads them up out of steerage, through second class. There is a close-up of a gate marked 'Second Class Only' which they open and go through. When a steward tries to stop them, they frighten him off and carry on. They proceed through the kitchens and find themselves in the first-class dining room. They halt, awe-struck, and there is a close-shot of Kate saying, wide-eyed, 'First-class'. But Murphy hastens them on and they get the women into the lifeboats.

Below, the steerage passengers begin to get restless and the captain orders guns to be distributed to the officers. A locked gate is broken

down with an axe by some steerage passengers, despite a steward threatening to have them arrested for damaging company property. Eventually
the steerage passengers are allowed through but find the lifeboats have
gone. Even in the lifeboats class attitudes persist. One upper-class woman
complains about a sailor smoking: 'People really ought to control themselves.' Another selfishly complains about being moved into another
lifeboat: 'I've had quite enough.' Lady Richard vetoes the idea of the
half-empty lifeboat returning for survivors: 'We're crowded enough as
it is. I'm feeling most unwell.' But by now all the classes are mingled in
the lifeboats. The sinking of the ship symbolizes the end of that very
structured society.

Given Baker's and MacQuitty's commitment to inclusivity and
authenticity in telling the story, David Lubin's comment on their treatment of the working-class figures is grotesquely misplaced. Lubin writes:

> In contrast to its reverent treatment of officers, *A Night to Remember*
> does not hesitate to mock or otherwise denigrate some of the lower-
> class seamen and stewards aboard the liner. After the collision the baker
> gets himself drunk and bumbles along comically, and a sailor ineptly
> wrestles with two collapsible deck-chairs that he attempts to tie together
> into his own private life-raft. One scurrilous seaman tries to make off
> with the chief purser's life preserver and is knocked unconscious for it,
> another beats away hapless swimmers who climb aboard his overturned
> lifeboat, while a third, a cockney quartermaster in charge of a lifeboat
> full of women, refuses Molly Brown's insistence that they row back to
> pick up survivors. This particular incident is repeated in *Titanic* and is
> the only occasion in that film in which a working-class figure is singled
> out for rebuke.[5]

This is wrong in almost every particular. There is no desire to belittle
or denigrate any working-class figure in *A Night to Remember*. All the
incidents that are dramatized actually happened on that fatal night and
are recorded in Walter Lord's book. Far from being denigrated, baker
Charles Joughin is being celebrated as an unlikely hero. He gives up his
place in a lifeboat to a lady. 'Ladies first, eh, sir,' he says to Lightoller,
when he could have stayed in the boat as one of the seamen needed to
man it. He then decides to insulate himself with whisky. When he is in
the water he holds on to the upturned boat until allowed to come aboard.
Throughout he is treated by the filmmakers with admiration. The sailor
trying to make his own life-raft is seen as an example of desperation and
is tragic rather than comic. Seamen did beat off hapless passengers and

refuse to return for survivors, for fear of swamping their boats. The incident of the stoker who stole the lifejacket from the wireless operator Phillips (not the chief purser) was reported by wireless officer Bride in a newspaper interview given immediately on arriving in New York. As for working-class characters not being rebuked in Cameron's *Titanic*, several stewards are clearly criticized for trying to hold back the steerage passengers. Denigration of the working classes was no part of the project of Baker, Ambler and MacQuitty.

NATION

Although Captain Smith does not say in this version, 'Be British', *A Night to Remember* is almost a British riposte to Fox's 1953 *Titanic*. In the Fox film all the passengers were American and included the historically authentic Astors, Strauses, Guggenheim, Molly Brown and George Widener. In *A Night to Remember* the passengers are overwhelmingly British. The Astors are completely omitted. The Strauses, Guggenheim, Molly Brown and Colonel Gracie all appear but in minor supporting roles. The composite characters (the Lucases and the Clarkes), while based in large part on Americans, are depicted as British. The American gambler Jay Yates is played as British. Asked why this was, Roy Baker concludes that it was because it was a British film made by British artists for a British audience. He was not conscious of any deliberate bid to exclude the Americans, and pointed to the presence of the authentic American characters, including Molly Brown ('a wonderful character'). He also points out that at the end as the ship finally went under, he included a sequence of shots of doomed passengers each praying in their own language, to demonstrate the multiplicity of nationalities on board.

But there is an overwhelmingly British feel to the film, in the reaction of the passengers and in the behaviour under stress. It is hard not to relate this to the Second World War. The war brought the idea of national identity into sharp focus. Books, essays and articles were pumped out defining and analysing the nature of Britishness. The British national character was deemed to be composed of a sense of humour, a sense of duty, a sense of stoicism, a sense of tolerance and a sense of individualism, which in the wartime situation was subordinated to a sense of community. The Ministry of Information laid down 'British life and character' as one of the objectives for propaganda and films played an important part in communicating this image. It was matched by the

emergence of a style of documentary authenticity in films which resulted
in an identifiable school of filmmaking that was recognized and praised
by critics. Dilys Powell wrote in 1947 about

> a new movement in the British cinema: the movement towards concentra-
> tion on the native subject, the movement towards documentary truth in
> the entertainment film. The war both encouraged a new seriousness of
> approach by British producers and directors, and drove them to look
> nearer home than before in their themes ... This mingling of docu-
> mentary technique and native character marks many British war films.
> [She concluded that] The semi-documentary film has gained a hold
> over British imaginations ... The British no longer demand pure fantasy
> from their films; they can be receptive also to the imaginative interpreta-
> tion of everyday life.[6]

One of the films she singled out as an exemplar of the new form was
In Which We Serve, which anticipated *A Night to Remember* by cutting
back and forth between the captain, the chief petty officer and an ordinary seaman and their families in the story of HMS *Torrin*, a British ship
sunk in the battle of Crete.

Roger Manvell detected the same trend in British films in the period
1942–45 and related it directly to the experience of the war:

> It is inevitable that the effects of a major catastrophe like the World War
> should transform the common material of every popular medium of
> expression ... Popular behaviour in this new war showed little desire for
> heroics and national self-display. Public speeches were for the most part
> toned down to expressions of solidarity and determination. When
> eventually the real war subjects began to be produced as distinct from
> ... melodramas ... this quiet sense of national feeling, this reticence and
> wry humour became part of the tradition which was to guide the concep-
> tion of the remarkable films of 1942–45 ... The British people went
> about the war as a difficult task to be worked off as efficiently as possible,
> and actions of unusual endurance or exceptional bravery were carried
> out as part of a routine. This desire for understatement developed as a
> regular attitude in the Services, and was faithfully put in the films by
> screen-writers, directors and actors only too conscious of the emotional
> implications, and the wider national significance of the stories they were
> representing ... Everyone knew something of war through the common
> experience of sons and daughters, husbands and lovers. Almost everyone
> knew the sound of bombing and the vivid state of tension before the

crash of explosion. The film producers were dealing with a psycho-logically aware audience. They could not afford ... to turn into melo-drama stories so close to the heart of Britain. Care was taken therefore to make the reconstruction of warfare on land, sea or in the air accurate to the conditions involved rather than spectacular for its own sake.[7]

The Way to the Stars (1945) was the last great film during the the war and was voted by *Daily Mail* readers the best film of the entire war. There was a remarkable critical consensus about its qualities. The critics almost universally praised the film for its realism, Englishness and emotional restraint. In a sense they were equating all three.[8] All that Powell, Manvell and the critics of *The Way to the Stars* wrote about wartime films could equally be applied to *A Night to Remember*. Emotion-ally it is very British.

Kenneth More's Lightoller with his good nature, sense of duty, decisiveness and natural authority is the ideal British hero. He supervises the filling of the lifeboats calmly and efficiently. He urges the passengers not to panic. He demonstrates both authority and seamanship in taking command of an upturned boat, calming those aboard it and steering it to safety. He is a blood-brother to those wartime British officers that he played in other films. All the officers behave well. Captain Smith puts the evacuation into effect with calmness and grim determination after designer Thomas Andrews has explained matter-of-factly the certainty that the ship will sink.

Duty is a continuing theme. Wireless Officer Phillips remains at his post transmitting SOS continually until the power has gone. Captain Smith then relieves the two wireless officers, saying, 'You've done your duty. You can do no more. It's every man for himself. I release you both. God bless you.' Wallace Hartley and his bandsmen play until the ship is on the point of plunging beneath the waves. 'It's the end, boys, we've done our duty. We can go,' he tells them. The engineers remain at their post to ensure that the lights survive for as long as possible. The chief engineer, with characteristic British phlegm, remarks, 'If any of you feel like praying, you'd better go ahead. The rest of you can join me in a cup of tea.' They too buckle down to their duty.

There is emotional restraint also among the passengers. It is the cardinal characteristic of Robert Lucas, as played by John Merivale. Lucas encounters Andrews, tells him he is not 'the panicking kind' but wants the truth. He is told that the ship has only an hour to live and he should get his wife and children off. Accepting his advice, Lucas even

ventures a joke: 'I take it you and I may be in the same boat later.'
Playing down the danger, he tells his wife that she and the children must
get into the lifeboat to conform with the company rules and the captain's
advice. He assures her it will only be for a while. He calmly fills his
cigar case and puts a necklace round her neck. He then escorts them to
the deck and gently persuades his wife and children into the boat. In one
of the most moving scenes in the film, Lucas kisses his sleeping son on
the forehead, says 'Goodbye, my dear son', and hands him into the
boat. This is done in medium-close shot and intercut with a shot of
Lightoller looking on sadly at this parting, a parting which both Lucas
and Lightoller know will be for ever. Baker thought this parting 'beautifully played' and there is indeed more genuine emotion concentrated in
this one scene than in the whole contrived, bloated and melodramatic
three hours of James Cameron's *Titanic*. The point about understatement and restraint is not lack of emotion, it is control of emotion. Good
actors like the ones in this scene, and in many other scenes in the film,
are able to suggest the emotion that is held in check and this sense of
restraint as a way of dealing with crisis and emergency is therefore
doubly moving. Like John Merivale as Lucas, Laurence Naismith as
Captain Smith and Michael Goodliffe as Andrews deliver classic performances of stoicism and emotional restraint.

As the ship goes down, a bearded man sits calmly reading in the
smoking room. He is never identified but *Titanic* buffs would know that
this is journalist W. T. Stead, whose last recorded moments were spent
in this way. The actor is made up to resemble Stead. Benjamin Guggenheim and his valet appear in evening suits and without lifejackets: 'We've
dressed now in our best and are prepared to go down like gentlemen.'
The valet nods his agreement: 'That is so, sir.' The 'we' here applies
both to the millionaire and his valet. Both are gentlemen in the face of
death. Miss Evans gives the last place on the last boat to a married
woman: 'You've got children waiting at home.'

Linked to the sense of Britishness evident throughout is a concern
with the burdens of command and the idea of responsibility. Baker's
final film for AKS had been *Think It Over*, aimed at teaching newly
promoted brigadiers how to think strategically. The nature of command,
the strains and stresses, the life-and-death decisions, the thought pro-
cesses of the men in charge are recurrent themes in the work of both
Ambler and Baker, particularly *Morning Departure*, *Passage Home*, *The
Cruel Sea* and *Yangtse Incident*. *A Night to Remember* is concerned with
the way in which the captain and the officers conduct themselves and

6. *Mr and Mrs Isidor Straus (Meier T\zelniker and Helen Misener).*

7. *Romance blossoms between emigrants below deck.*

8. *Robert Lucas (John Merivale), devoted husband and father, persuades his wife (Honor Blackman) and children to leave the ship by pretending that there is nothing serious happening.*

6–9. *Gender: the film stressed marriage, family and heterosexual romance.*

carry out their duties during the disaster. It also focuses on Captain Rostron, his seamanship and preparations for picking up survivors.

Given this recurrent interest in responsibility, it is instructive to note what Baker sees as Ismay's motivation in this context. He thought that the role was 'played absolutely brilliantly by Frank Lawton. He got the character – the panic, the shame and the guilt.' But Baker has his own view of why Ismay entered the lifeboat rather than staying on board to go down with the ship along with the captain and the designer: 'Both Lawton and I felt that he knew that he had to go back and face the music. I couldn't believe that a man in his position with his responsibility would not have known that and would want to face his responsibility.'[9] This of course contrasts with the view of many commentators both in Britain and America then and since who have accused Ismay of wanting to save his own skin, at all costs. But it conforms exactly to Baker's world-view in which responsibility is a key element.

There is a prevailing tone of irony throughout. Irony, which is known to be a British characteristic, derives in this case from the audience's foreknowledge of the fate of the ship. So when at the outset the ship is christened with the traditional hope, 'May God bless her and all who sail in her', this is known to be a vain hope as the ship will sink. When Dr O'Loughlin proposes a toast to Andrews ('Good health'), we know that he is going down with the ship and will not enjoy that good health. When the captain realizes that the lifeboats will hold fewer than half the passengers, he remarks to Andrews with grim irony: 'I don't think the Board of Trade regulations visualized this situation, do you?' When Bride suggests that Phillips use the new signal SOS, joking, 'It may be your last chance to use it', he is unwittingly prophetic as Phillips will not be among the survivors. When Lightoller reprimands Ismay for interfering and a seaman remarks to a colleague, 'There'll be trouble about that when we get to New York', we know, as they do not, that many of them will not get to New York. At the end, when the *Californian* contacts the *Carpathia* offering help, Captain Rostron replies: 'All that was humanly possible has been done'. In fact, this is the supreme irony, for all that was humanly possible had not been done. The *Californian*, if it had acted, might have saved many more lives than the *Carpathia* was able to.

GENDER

Above all, the film is an overwhelming endorsement of marriage. At the outset Lightoller and his wife are shown to enjoy a happy marriage. During the disaster, Mrs Straus famously opts to stay with Mr Straus: 'We've always lived together – so why should I leave him now,' she says. 'Where you go, I go.' When Colonel Gracie suggests that no one would object to an old gentleman like Mr Straus going in the boat with his wife, Mr Straus says: 'I will not go before the other men.' 'We stay,' says Mrs Straus proudly. They will go down together. Hearing this, the Clarkes, the honeymooning couple, say, 'We started out together; we'll finish together,' and are killed by the falling funnel. Robert Lucas, persuading his wife to go, says (using the words actually spoken by Lucien P. Smith to his wife): 'I never expected to ask you to obey me, but this is one time you must. It is only a matter of form to have women and children first. I'll catch a later boat.' Mrs Lucas goes with the children.

RELIGION

The consolatory role of religion plays its part in *A Night to Remember* as it did in the previous film versions. 'God bless you,' says the captain to the wireless officers as he relieves them of their duty. 'God bless you', says a wife being parted from her husband as the evacuation begins. 'Good luck, God bless you,' shouts doomed gambler Jay Yates as he swims away from the upturned lifeboat. When the band plays 'Nearer, My God, to Thee', with the cellist singing, there is a succession of reaction shots as the inevitability of the tragedy is confirmed. We later hear it on the soundtrack as passengers huddled at the stern of the sinking ship recite the Lord's Prayer each in their own language just before the final plunge. There is a memorial service aboard the *Carpathia*. We hear 'Nearer, My God, to Thee' again on the soundtrack after Captain Rostron replies to the message from the *Californian* offering help, 'All that was humanly possible has been done.'

ETHNICITY

New to *A Night to Remember* and a pointer to the future is the prominence of the Irish emigrants in steerage. There had been steerage passengers in the 1943 and 1953 *Titanic* but they had not been Irish. *A Night to Remember* is the first *Titanic* film to accord the Irish their historical role as a significant presence among the third-class passengers. Baker, Ambler and MacQuitty did so in the interests of authenticity; but their prominence in *S.O.S. Titanic* and the 1997 *Titanic* had a distinct ideological purpose.

Britain had traditionally been the biggest foreign market for US films and one of the reasons Hollywood produced pro-British and pro-empire films in the 1930s, 1940s and 1950s was to keep British audiences happy. By the 1960s, mass cinema closures in Britain and a general decline in cinema-going meant that Britain was no longer the lucrative market it had once been for American films. Since then Hollywood has no longer cared what British audiences think or feel and the British in general and the British Empire in particular have become convenient all-purpose villains, the antithesis of the democratic, classless, liberal, multi-ethnic, equal opportunities culture that is the ideal of post-1960s Hollywood. The British Empire, which in Hollywood's heyday had been depicted as very largely benevolent, wise and well-intentioned, is now seen as exclusively snobbish, racist, cruel and exploitative. When in need of a

9. *Wireless operator John Phillips (Kenneth Griffith) stays at his post until the end.*

10. *Chairman Bruce Ismay (Frank Lawton) saves his life by escaping in a lifeboat with the women and children.*

11. *Professional gamblers Hoyle (Redmond Phillips) and Yates (Ralph Michael) meet different ends: Hoyle escapes in a half-filled lifeboat, Yates swims away from an upturned boat so as not to overload it.*

12. *Robert Lucas (John Merivale) hands over his sleeping son to Second Officer Lightoller (Kenneth More) and remains on board to go down with the ship.*

9–12. *Duty and selfishness: both devotion to duty and the desire for self-preservation can be seen among some passengers and some crew.*

sneering, supercilious and sadistic villain, Hollywood now turns largely to British, or more specifically English, actors.

Conversely, the Irish are regularly used as the symbols of and opponents of British imperial oppression, and when a spokesman for Hollywood's modern values is needed in an historical film, he is more often than not depicted as Irish, as for instance in *The Mountains of the Moon*, *Zulu Dawn* and *The Ghost and the Darkness*. Ireland is everybody's favourite little country, the democratic David which defied and defeated the British imperial Goliath. All of this ideological baggage is carried by the Irish emigrants in *S.O.S. Titanic* and the 1997 *Titanic*, their democratic, classless credentials established by their spontaneous singing and dancing, breaking down of locked gates and defiance of the English officer class.

FOUR
Post-Production

A Night to Remember was premièred at the Odeon, Leicester Square, on 3 July 1958. Among the audience were ten survivors of the *Titanic*, five passengers and five crew members.[1] It received some of the best reviews ever of any Rank film.

The popular press was almost universally ecstatic. Recalling the reception of *Morning Departure*, the praise concentrated on the documentary authenticity of the account and the fact that this was a British achievement. Ernest Betts in *The People* (6 July 1958), heading the review, 'This film is unsinkable', declared: 'This tremendous picture tells you what movie success is made of. It's the answer to the dismal Jimmies in Wardour Street who are always croaking about a dying industry ... While the British film industry can turn out pictures of this calibre, it's unthinkable that it should be sinkable. This is a film to remember.' Harold Conway in the *Daily Sketch* (3 July 1958) thought it the finest of all the *Titanic* films and declared: 'It claims high place among Britain's greatest pictures.' Peter Burnup in the *News of the World* (6 July 1958), calling it 'a film to remember', said the film added 'new lustre to the British film industry'. Jympson Harman in the *Evening News* (3 July 1958) proclaimed it 'a magnificent milestone in the efforts of British film to improve on the mighty American variety', and said, 'never from Hollywood have I seen such perfect realism in recreating a shipwreck'.

The critics in the main agreed that the film's strength lay in its meticulous documentary re-creation of the disaster in all its aspects. Ernest Betts in the *People* predicted certain box-office success, for three reasons:

1. Because it's real – every scene hits you with a deadly and exciting realism.

2. Because it's brilliantly acted and directed. Kenneth More stars effectively, but he can't outstar the ship. She's a ship with a ready-made Oscar.

3. Because it's big in every way – in emotion, conflict, drama, suspense, action and spectacle. It takes you aboard to the heart of the disaster.

Campbell Dixon in the *Daily Telegraph* (5 July 1958) thought the film 'shows that the subject has lost none of its enthralling interest, that the truth is less familiar than one had supposed, and that the previous films were even more gratuitously bogus than they seemed to be at the time'. Harry Weaver in the *Daily Herald* (4 July 1958) thought it had 'a harsh reality that grips and numbs as it unfolds – without passion – the tragic story'. It gave you the feeling, 'I was there'. Frank Jackson of *Reynolds News* (6 July 1958) said it 'gripped him from start to finish' and 'gave him food for thought long after the lights had gone up'. Elizabeth Frank in the *News Chronicle* (4 July 1958) thought it 'in every way a magnificent piece of film making', and said: 'Where the film succeeds brilliantly is in the believable behaviour of everyone concerned. There is not one moment of false dramatics and the hundreds of players emerge as individual personalities.' The *Manchester Guardian* (5 July 1958) said: 'It may in fact have been much like this. The film, though very big, is intentionally plain ... it does not reduce itself to melodrama, it covers a multitude of factual aspects of the disaster ... it allows the drama to develop, as it were, of its own true and considerable impetus.' It was, said the paper, 'typical and creditable that it did not put its stress on stars'.

Leonard Mosley in the *Daily Express* (4 July 1958) found it a 'shattering film to watch' and said it 'reconstructs with lavish and moving attention to detail the sinking'. Peter Burnup in the *News of the World* (6 July 1958) said: 'I defy any man or woman to remain unmoved.' *The Times* (2 July 1958) thought 'the strength of the film lies in the acute sense of participation which it arouses in the audience as the mounting tension which it creates and the crowd scenes at the end have been filmed with terrifying realism'. *Time and Tide* (12 July 1958) thought it 'a very good film indeed. The strength of the work lies in the acute sense of participation it arouses in the audience. We are there.'

The fact that the *Titanic* was still in 1958 a disaster within living memory was brought home strikingly by the very personal review by Dilys Powell in the *Sunday Times* (6 July 1958):

Perhaps it is good for one to be forced to recall the Titanic ... of all the horrors conferred on us by the age of speed and comfort the most appalling to me is still the sinking of R.M.S. Titanic, and I should not unless driven let myself think of it. No doubt this is irrational. I ought to be shrinking much more from the thought of Belsen or Hiroshima ...

No use: the story of the Titanic still has an effect which none of the tortures or massacres of the past twenty years can equal. It is doubtful whether anybody who was not alive in 1912 can know this feeling. It belongs to the period; to share it you did not have to be old enough to understand the news, you simply had to be there. A child in an orderly provincial household, at the time I scarcely grasped the facts ... Yet the sense of shock in the family affected me as it must have affected hundreds of thousands of my generation. The disaster, I told myself, was clearly too horrible to dwell on. I still don't want to know any more about the Titanic.

But she had been forced for professional reasons to review *A Night to Remember* and she found it 'a very good film':

As a feat of reconstruction this is a brilliant film, and by reconstruction I do not mean simply the rebuilding of the physical setting ... though the work of the art director, Alex Vetchinsky, and the technicians concerned must be regarded as extraordinary. I mean the fitting together of the incidents, the fragments of talk, which Mr. Lord's researches among survivors and contemporary reports have recovered for us ... There has been no attempt to dress up the tragedy. The recorded cowardice is here as well as the recorded bravery ... and the social climate is here. In the confusion of catastrophe the steerage passengers were almost forgotten ... The odious distinction belongs to the end of an age. Other aspects, too, of the story, are part of an end: the dissolution of a kind of confidence, a kind of optimism, the end of absolute faith in absolute safety. Perhaps my father and mother ... were vaguely conscious that the ground beneath their feet was no longer as solid as they had fancied. Perhaps this first intimation of insecurity it was which made, and still makes, the sinking of the Titanic so terrible to me and my contemporaries. At any rate after two world wars one is inclined, looking back at the night of April 14, 1912, to take it as a savage warning bell.

Several critics commented that the *Titanic* was the real star of the film (*Daily Mail, News of the World, Time and Tide, The Times*). But there was also praise for the production team. Fred Majdalany in the *Daily Mail* (4 July 1958), calling it 'an intelligent spectacle', thought More 'excellent', Ambler's script 'tight' and Baker's direction 'masterly'. Peter Burnup in the *News of the World* thought More gave 'one of the finest performances of his career'. The *Sunday Express* (6 July 1958) thought it 'brilliantly made' and directed with 'enormous flair and confidence'.

13. *Although the film prided itself on its factual accuracy, this launching ceremony never in fact took place. Designer Thomas Andrews (Michael Goodliffe) and Chairman Bruce Ismay (Frank Lawton) flank the unnamed lady.*

14. *Spectacular re-creation of the flooding of the engine rooms.*

15. *Whether or not the*
     steerage passengers
     were locked below
     decks and, if so,
     why is still hotly
     disputed.

16. *Kenneth More as Lightoller evacuating passengers. His character*
     was given several actions performed by other officers on the night.

13–16. *Factual accuracy (1)*

Dilys Powell in the *Sunday Times* thought More 'excellent'. The *Daily Telegraph's* Campbell Dixon thought it 'ably produced' and 'directed with an eye for telling detail by Roy Baker', and containing good performances by More 'and a score of others'. C. A. Lejeune in the *Observer* (6 July 1958) declared: 'Roy Baker handles the huge work of direction like a veteran, and I doubt if Eric Ambler has ever written a more nicely calculated screenplay. As a clean-cut, unbiased, dramatic presentation of a momentous fact in history, the British film seldom did a better job than this.' David Robinson in the *Financial Times* (7 July 1958) thought the staging was 'exemplary' and that 'the director ... and art director ... have subtly caught the feeling of the period'.

There were a few dissenting voices. William Whitebait in the *New Statesman* (12 July 1958) while conceding its documentary authenticity, reported, 'It doesn't thrill, it doesn't appal' and thought 'it evaded the whole social theme'. He evidently wanted a more robust and comprehensive denunciation of the upper classes. Philip Oakes in the *Sunday Dispatch* (6 July 1958) thought it 'worthy, well meant and ultimately dull', and said that after two previous film versions there was 'nothing in this version to justify a third retelling'. He thought the 'documentary detail impressive enough' but believed the 'men and women are submerged beneath a welter of facts'. David Robinson in the *Financial Times* (7 July 1958) thought it authentic in its 'harshness' but too fragmentary and episodic to sustain a two-hour film. Derek Hill in *Tribune* (12 July 1958), declaring roundly 'The Titanic won't keep British films off the rocks', thought it craftsmanlike but perceived 'a great gulf between the years of research into detail' and 'the conventional approach to the subject'. He thought it cliché-ridden and largely unconvincing. Nina Hibbin in the *Daily Worker* (5 June 1958) thought it a 'painstaking and sober reconstruction of a disaster which, quite clearly, should never have happened', but thought it 'lacking the imaginative personal touch' and found it 'occasionally repetitive and a little tedious'. They were a distinct minority but their reservations mostly related to the nature of the film as docu-drama.

It is instructive to compare the critical reaction to *A Night to Remember* with that enjoyed by the 1953 *Titanic*. Many of the critics were devastatingly dismissive of the 1953 *Titanic*. Almost all began their reviews with an account of the tragedy, and the fact that it still resonated in the popular memory is one of the reasons why the critical reaction was so hostile. Richard Winnington in the *News Chronicle* (20 June 1953) wrote in a review headed 'Titanically trivial': 'Confronted with the immensity

of this sudden dreadful climax to human fallibility, they have taken
refuge in cabin-trunk drama. The sinking of the Titanic embalms a cosy
box-office message.' The message was the triumph of young love and
the superiority of healthy Americanism to continental snobbery. He
complained that the *Titanic* itself 'plays a subsidiary part'.

Philip Hope-Wallace in the *Manchester Guardian* (20 June 1953) denounced the film as 'a farrago of second-rate melodramatics' and wrote:
'Forty years on, and the sinking of the Titanic still provides such an
overwhelming instance of tragic irony that one cannot even now read
unmoved the simple and terrible facts of the disaster. Was it too much
to hope that the film industry for the second time exploiting the dramatic
and fictional angles of the story, should do it decently? It was.'

Paul Holt in the *Daily Herald* (19 June 1953) took the same line,
heading his story 'Hollywood Can't Stick to the Truth'. He complained
that Hollywood had introduced into the true story of 'the most terrible
tragedy of the steamship era' a fictional plot that was 'highly improb-
able'. Why does Hollywood distrust the truth? he asked, answering: 'Is
it because they have grown so proud, after a quarter of a century of
success, that a true tale of tragedy is now too small for them and they
must invent their own? Or is it that they ceased to trust their audiences
to respond, and so press harder and harder on in search of an artificial
stimulant to sensation.' Reg Whitley in the *Daily Mirror* (19 June 1953)
called it 'a dull story about irritating people' and, apart from the 'spectacle of the vessel sinking ... in the final scenes', he found the film
'boring'.

William Whitebait in the *New Statesman* (27 June 1953) suggested
that the discerning cinema-goer leave after the first shots of the iceberg
at the beginning, 'because what follows is a let-down with hardly even
minor shock or pleasures'. He dismissed it as 'cheap fiction' and concluded: 'With the images of iceberg and liner, and the facts of the case,
a first-rate film could have been – and still could be – made.'

Another group of critics, while almost universally dismissing the
fictional elements, praised the factual elements of the film. Elspeth Grant
in *Time and Tide* (27 June 1953) found the story 'artificial, trivial and
strictly unmemorable' but admitted, 'the tremendous drama is admirably
handled in the factual part of the film, Mr. Negulesco's direction im-
aginatively pointing moments of menace and terror', and denounced
'the unworthy fiction that goes with it'. *The Times* (17 June 1953),
heading its review 'The Foundering of the Titanic', found the film only
'passable', denouncing the 'paltry fiction' of the main plot, but adding:

17.   *Kenneth More as Lightoller attempts to prevent panicking passengers swamping the lifeboats.*

18.   *Captain Rostron (Anthony Bushell) orders the* Carpathia *to steam to the aid of the* Titanic.

19. *The ship's orchestra play music to calm the passengers.*

20. *The* Titanic *sinks.*

17–20. *Factual accuracy (2)*

'What is excellent in it is the factual, or documentary, part which is based on evidence given at the inquiry.'

The *Evening News* (18 June 1953), while finding it 'regrettable that the world's greatest maritime disaster should be made the subject of commercial entertainment', thought *Titanic* 'one of the best pictures to come from America for some time'. But the critic felt the fictional plot 'small beer when you know that a bigger human tragedy is to come. On its more factual side, the film is excellent ... the whole thing is presented with reserve and absence of melodramatics.' Milton Schulman in the *Evening Standard* (18 June 1953) thought 'the documentary aspect of the sinking is told with a minimum of heroics and hysteria' and that the sinking was 'a most impressive and awesome spectacle'. He went on, 'The realism is in refreshing contrast to the unconvincing private lives of the Titanic's passengers', and concluded that the film 'sails an erratic course between authenticity and embarrassment'.

The Star (19 June 1953), having recounted the events of the tragedy, declared: 'To see those events depicted on the screen with such realism is moving and thrilling indeed. Technically the film is a wonderful achievement ... such reconstruction a remarkable feat.' It continued, 'Strange to think though that the disaster serves as nothing more than a background of a commonplace story', but concluded, 'It is the background that matters – the record of a pitiful event contrived with such realistic detail. Many people were in tears when I saw the film and I must confess that I was much moved by that part of it.'

Leonard Mosley of the *Daily Express* (19 June 1953) thought the end 'the best sea-disaster sequence ever filmed', but added 'in between Hollywood has inserted another of those routine domestic dramas'. Cecil Wilson in the *Daily Mail* (19 June 1953) thought the personal drama 'strikes a thin and artificial note' and the dialogue retains 'its glossy unreality' throughout, but he praised Negulesco for directing the scenes of the sinking 'with sensitive restraint' and thought the reaction of the passengers at the end was 'movingly conveyed'.

Thomas Spencer in the *Daily Worker* (20 June 1953) felt that 'all the elements of drama are there for the makers of *Titanic* without need to distort the facts', and thought the factual side of the film fine, but 'where the film falls down is in the collection of witless stuffed dummies who are trotted out in front of this fine factual background to provide that "human interest" without which we presumably could not be expected to sit without yawning through the story of the most dramatic shipwreck that ever happened'.

21. *Second Officer Lightoller (Kenneth More) and Colonel Gracie (James Dyrenforth) try to make sense of the tragedy.*

Only a couple of critics broke ranks. Campbell Dixon of the *Daily Telegraph* (20 June 1953) found it 'one of the most moving of all stories of the sea', and Virginia Graham in *The Spectator* (19 June 1953) thought it 'brilliantly directed ... a perfectly excellent picture, finely balanced between fact and fiction, stocked with plausible characters, working up quietly but strongly to its shattering climax which is, in effect, one of the most moving and dramatic half-hours I have ever sat through'.

What runs through the reviews is a demand for factual authenticity, a distaste for melodrama and in some cases an undisguised hostility towards Hollywood for tampering with the facts of a tragedy that was felt to be the common property of the audience. Only one critic – Milton Schulman of the *Evening Standard* – commented on the fact that all the passengers on the *Titanic* were American, and one critic – Campbell Dixon – thought the film had been 'generous to us Britons'. The hostility was more towards Hollywood fiction than American bias.

The reaction of the New York critics was more favourable. The *New York Times* praised 'the sometimes moving and often exciting drama'; *The News* praised direction and acting; and *The Mirror* a 'drama of taut emotions, grippingly told with a high element of suspense'.[2] But some of the more discriminating magazines shared the distaste of the British critics. *Time* (24 April 1953) which thought 'Too much time is spent on contrived fiction, too little on dramatic fact', found the fictional element 'melodramatic' although 'glossily put together and smoothly acted'. John McCarten in the *New Yorker* (6 June 1953) thought the *Titanic* tragedy 'indisputably one of the most fascinating and terrifying in maritime history, and it would be almost impossible to so distort the facts of the matter that catastrophe is reduced to the dimensions of a comic strip. But in Hollywood nothing is impossible.' He went on to call the *Titanic* 'a bilious combination of brummagem melodrama and synthetic escapes', and while conceding that 'the actors performed competently in standard *Grand Hotel* style', added 'but they never succeed in lifting the business above the mediocre'.

The respective critical reactions to *Titanic* and *A Night to Remember* conform precisely to the dominant critical ethic of the 1940s and 1950s identified by John Ellis after a thorough analysis of a broad range of newspaper and journal reviews. This critical stance is one which placed the greatest value on documentary realism, literary quality and a middle-class improvement ethic and was particularly critical of melodrama, fantasy and horror.[3] The British critics then accepted *A Night to Remember* on its own terms as an authentic and truth-telling docu-drama produced in the style of sober realism that had emerged from the war as the best and finest form of cinematic production.

THE AMERICAN RELEASE

A Night to Remember was released in America in late 1958 and received reviews which in many cases echoed the praise bestowed by the British papers. *Time* magazine (5 January 1959) admired the documentary style of the film and said that Baker and Ambler 'have skilfully paced and developed the onrush of disaster, and have also managed to involve the spectator's feelings with those of the doomed men and women'. The influential trade paper *Variety*, commenting like the British critics that 'the ship itself is the star', praised the 'impressive, almost documentary flavour' of the staging, and went on:

> The errors and confusion which played a part in the drama are brought out with no whitewashing. Although many of the passengers and crew come vividly to life, there is no attempt to hang a fictional story on any of them. Technically, director Roy Baker does a superb job in difficult circumstances. His direction of some of the panic scenes during the manning of the lifeboats ... is masterly. Eric Ambler's screenplay ... without skimping the nautical side of the job, brings out how some people kept their heads and others became cowards.[4]

The *Motion Picture Herald* (20 December 1958) called it 'a tremendous film, intelligent, authentic and, above all, moving and exciting'. Hollis Alpert in the *Saturday Review* (13 December 1958) praised the detailed reconstruction and 'crisp' direction of Roy Baker but wondered if 'audiences care enough to justify this much work'. This last ominous comment was prophetic.

The New York critics gave the film rave reviews. Bosley Crowther in the *New York Times* (17 December 1958), calling the film 'as fine and convincing an enactment as anyone could wish – or expect', said, 'this remarkable picture is a brilliant and moving account of the behaviour of the people on the *Titanic* on that night'. But there was a three-day newspaper strike at the crucial period and fewer people than usual saw the reviews. The favourable critical reception in America culminated in *A Night to Remember* receiving the 1958 Golden Globe award of the Hollywood Foreign Press Association as Best English Language Foreign Film, and being voted one of the five best foreign films of 1958 by the National Board of Review.

This did not, however, translate into audience attendance. MacQuitty spent a month in the United States in early 1959 promoting the film in vain. He attributed the film's failure to attract audiences to the lack of stars and the unpopularity of the docu-drama format with the mass audience raised in and conditioned by Hollywood melodramatic fictions.[5]

The attempts to drum up audiences provoked controversy. The *Daily Herald* (6 December 1958) reported shock in New York over a publicity gimmick – the distribution of cocktail swizzle sticks in the form of the *Titanic*, which were to rest on the ice in cocktail glasses and to sink as the ice melted. 'Even publicity-conscious Americans are shocked,' reported the newspaper. The Rank Organization issued a statement: 'This is an idea of our New York office who have sole responsibility for promotional activities they consider suitable for the American market.'

Kenneth More thought there was a more sinister reason for the film's comparative lack of success in the United States. He complained that his British hit films such as *Reach for the Sky* and *A Night to Remember* 'received good coverage, but not good distribution' in the United States. The problem with *Reach for the Sky* was that 'Americans did not want to know about British war heroes', and with *A Night to Remember*, 'critics praised it but because it had been made in Britain with British capital, that was sufficient to damn it'. He contrasted this with another black-and-white maritime movie in which he starred, *Sink the Bismarck* (1960), which made 'considerable profit in the United States, largely because American money was behind it'.[6] The failure of the American industry to promote British films had been a perennial complaint of the British industry. If More is correct, a combination of the form, the subject matter and the exclusively British origin of the film sealed its fate with American audiences.

THE BOX-OFFICE RECEPTION

Precise box-office returns for the film are not available. *Kinematograph Weekly* (18 December 1958) reported that the top British box-office films of the year were *Bridge on the River Kwai*, *Dunkirk*, *The Vikings* and *Carry On Sergeant*. *A Night to Remember* is one of thirty-eight other films described as being 'in the money'. The *Motion Picture Herald* (17 January 1959) confirms *Kwai*, *Dunkirk* and *The Vikings* as the top British box-office attractions with *A Night to Remember* among the fourteen next big money-makers. Roy Baker lamented in 2001: 'I'm still told by Bill [MacQuitty] that our film has yet to go into profit.' He explained that the original huge budget, the comparative lack of success in America and the downbeat nature of the story ('People were coming out of the cinema in tears') may help to explain the lack of profitability. MacQuitty attributes it mainly to Rank's accounting procedures. The budget for the film was borrowed at interest and the film was marketed as part of a package of ten films. Rank regularly offset the profits of *A Night to Remember* against the interest payments and the losses of the other films in the package.[7]

LATER ANALYSES OF THE FILM

Although both producer William MacQuitty and director Roy Baker saw their film as a detailed and precise documentary re-creation of a specific historical event and contemporary critics received it in the same spirit, it is impossible in retrospect to divorce it from its historical context. The film was released towards the end of the 1950s, a decade which critics have seen as one of 'complacency and inertia', as 'extraordinarily dead', as a 'doldrums era'. The post-war Labour government had introduced the welfare state, nationalized key industries and given independence to India. But rationing, shortages and restrictions persisted. The generation which had won the war wanted the welfare state but they also wanted fun and spending money and in 1951 elected a Conservative government, which was to remain in office for thirteen years by maintaining the welfare state but dismantling restrictions, ending rationing and promoting affluence. The first half of the 1950s was a period of peace, prosperity and order. The crime rate was falling, there was full employment and rising productivity. The greater availability of consumer durables blunted class antagonisms. As Vernon Bogdanor and Robert Skidelsky wrote in 1970: 'Perhaps the period of Conservative rule will be looked back upon as the last period of quiet before the storm, rather like the Edwardian age which in some respects it resembles. In that case its tranquillity may well come to be valued more highly than its omissions.'[8]

Just as the Second World War had energized British society, so it revitalized and stimulated the British film industry. That industry ran out of steam at about the same time as the Labour government. Many of the great directors of the 1940s (David Lean, Carol Reed, Michael Powell, Thorold Dickinson, Robert Hamer, Alexander MacKendrick) went into decline, retired or moved to America. Two of the great studios of the 1940s, Ealing and Gainsborough, ceased film production and were sold to television. There was a sclerotic sense of old formulae being unimaginatively followed, of a failure of nerve and invention. The characteristic products of the decade reflected this: the war films that sought to relive old glories, the Norman Wisdom comedies that trod in the footsteps of George Formby, the celebrations of empire, and the largely anaemic 'international' epics which aimed futilely to break into the American market.

Then in the years 1956–58 came a cultural watershed, energizing society with a cultural revolt which was to lead in due course to the end

of Conservative rule, the return to office of Labour and the birth of the
'swinging sixties'. The later 1950s saw, on the political front, the Suez
debacle and the Notting Hill race riots, symptoms of Britain's emergence
into a post-imperial, post-Victorian world. But the period also saw the
arrival of rock music from the United States, the appearance of the
'angry young men' of literature and the theatre and the first steps
towards the development of a distinctive youth culture that was to flower
in the 1960s.

Cinematically this cultural watershed was represented by the British
'New Wave' films which began with *Room at the Top* (1959) and *Look
Back in Anger* (1959) and dramatized the discontents of the working-
class young, Hammer horror films which began with *The Curse of
Frankenstein* (1956) and *Dracula* (1958) pointing up the ordered bourgeois
normality of Victorian England and the forces of unreason and excess
lurking below the surface, and the Carry On films which began with
Carry On Sergeant (1958) and initiated a twenty-year campaign of defiance against the established canons of taste, decency, decorum and
respectability.

Coinciding exactly with these films comes *A Night to Remember*,
which Raymond Durgnat was perhaps the first critic to see chiming
with the national mood in the late 1950s. Durgnat explicitly links it with
one of the other box-office successes of 1958, *Dunkirk*. With three of
the stars of Roy Baker's *Morning Departure* (John Mills, Richard Attenborough and Bernard Lee), its realism, pessimism and grimly authentic
re-creation of a maritime evacuation, which gave the spectator the
feeling of actually being present, suggest that *Dunkirk* might easily have
been directed by Baker. It was in fact directed by Leslie Norman but it
shares much of the mood and ethos of *A Night to Remember* and *Morning
Departure*. Durgnat wrote:

> The English pride themselves in losing every battle except the last, and
> the underlying guilt behind this became conspicuous in two films pro-
> duced in 1958, Leslie Norman's *Dunkirk* and Roy Baker's *A Night to
> Remember*. Not only the *Titanic* in 1912 but Britain's titanic complacency
> is holed below the waterline. Both these films possess real moral tragedy
> and beauty, precisely because they admit some cynicism is justified.[9]

Coming as it did on the eve of the 1960s and the profound cultural
revolution that overthrew not only aristocratic but middle-class values
and assumptions, *A Night to Remember* has inevitably been seen by some
subsequent critics as a critique of the class system of post-war Britain,

despite the statements to the contrary of both director and producer.[10]

Richard Howells, contrasting *A Night to Remember* with the essentially classless 1953 Hollywood *Titanic*, sees the 1958 film as articulating 'a readjustment of British class values and attitudes in a post-war era'. It is, he argues, a response to welfare state Britain. It does not fundamentally criticize or even question the system but rather attitudes within it and it views the whole question from a middle-class perspective, particularly through the person of Lightoller as the calm and dedicated middle-class professional.[11]

David M. Lubin, writing from an American perspective, sees *A Night to Remember* as 'a Cold War fable about the need for preparedness and competent military and class leadership', and points out:

> The chief focus of the film is not the many private tragedies and sorrowful partings that occur but rather the unfortunate communications foulups and lack of preparedness that led to such an unnecessary loss of life. Indeed ... *A Night to Remember* seems concerned above all with issues of coded communication, miscommunication, bungled communication and garbled communication. Numerous scenes take place in the offices of the wireless operators on the *Titanic*; and two other ships, the nearby *Californian* and the 50-mile-away *Carpathia* ... Obviously, the obsession with miscommunication and failed warning systems was a meaningful concern to a nation of filmgoers who only a dozen or so years before had relied heavily upon early-warning systems in order to survive the nightly blitz ... In 1956 the British government installed a new early-warning system against nuclear attack ... Here was a context in which *A Night to Remember*'s concern with safety and communication was timely and meaningful. In *Titanic*, by contrast, it's barely a side issue.[12]

This may, however, be a function more of form than content. *A Night to Remember* is a docu-drama largely dealing with the last two hours of the ship's life, when desperate communication was to the fore; the 1997 *Titanic* is a romantic melodrama covering the whole voyage and focusing on the experiences of one young couple.

My own view is, as I have been making clear, that it is more plausible to relate *A Night to Remember* in form and content to the Second World War. It was the work of three men who had been through the war, had experienced the lowering of class barriers that occurred under the impact of the war, had observed the conduct of people under stress. Consciously or unconsciously, *A Night to Remember* could be seen as an allegory of Britain experiencing the impact of the Second World War, the class-structured world not just of 1912 but of 1939 being punctured by the iceberg. Then, during the crisis, trained officers like Lightoller take charge and decent men and women of all backgrounds behave well under fire. For as in the 1953 Hollywood *Titanic*, the ideological elements of the myth (chivalric conduct, the primacy of marriage, the consolidating role of religion) are all affirmed in *A Night to Remember*.

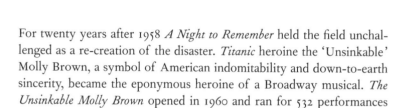

FIVE
The *Titanic* and the Cinema: After *A Night to Remember*

For twenty years after 1958 *A Night to Remember* held the field unchallenged as a re-creation of the disaster. *Titanic* heroine the 'Unsinkable' Molly Brown, a symbol of American indomitability and down-to-earth sincerity, became the eponymous heroine of a Broadway musical. *The Unsinkable Molly Brown* opened in 1960 and ran for 532 performances with Tammy Grimes and Harve Presnell in the leads. It was filmed by MGM in 1964 with Debbie Reynolds and Harve Presnell. It became the third highest grossing film of the year, taking $7.5 million.

Molly Brown was characterized as one of those exhaustingly high-spirited Western musical heroines like Calamity Jane and Annie 'Get Your Gun' Oakley. She sang, danced, bellowed and wisecracked her way through a 'rags to riches' populist fable in which feisty, plain-talking Missouri tomboy Molly Tobin marries simple, cheerful, virile Colorado miner Johnny Brown. They strike gold and become millionaires but are snubbed by the snobs of Denver society for their rough-hewn ways. They retreat to Europe to acquire culture but a return to Denver results in another social debacle. Molly returns to Europe but Johnny, tired of life away from America, remains at home. Eventually homesick for America, Molly, like Barbara Stanwyck in *Titanic* (1953), embarks on the *Titanic*. The *Titanic* disaster sequences were lifted wholesale from that 1953 Fox *Titanic*. After the sinking, Molly cheers up the survivors in her lifeboat, arrives in America to find she has become a heroine and is reunited with Johnny and welcomed by the Denver snobs.

Then in 1979 came *S.O.S. Titanic*. It was the first account of the disaster to be made in colour. Jean Negulesco had wanted to shoot his version in colour but Fox had vetoed this on grounds of cost. Rank Film Distributors had wanted *A Night to Remember* shot in Technicolor and Vistavision but MacQuitty had refused in the interests of authenticity.[1]

S.O.S. Titanic was a joint venture of ABC-Television in America and the British film company EMI. It resulted in a 140-minute television film for showing in the USA and an edited 109-minute version for cinematic release in Britain. It was directed by an experienced television director Billy Hale, whose previous feature films had been 'B' Westerns (*Gunfight in Abilene, Journey to Shiloh*), and it was scripted by Emmy-award-winning screenwriter James Costigan. This version decided to cover the whole voyage rather than just the last night. Asked why a new version was needed, co-executive producer William S. Gilmore Jr described *A Night to Remember* as 'a parochial British film'. The new film unwisely laid claim to greater authenticity than the earlier version, declaring its script to be based on 'factual and personal accounts' of the disaster and research by the Titanic Historical Society.[2] Captain Smith accurately declares that *Titanic* had no formal naming ceremony, but the film succeeds in getting the date of the disaster wrong, flashing up April 12, 1912 instead of April 14.

The film begins with Bruce Ismay giving a guided tour of the ship and the characters include the familiar figures of Captain Smith and his officers, Wireless Officers Bride and Phillips, Bandmaster Wallace Hartley, Thomas Andrews, the Astors, Benjamin Guggenheim, Molly Brown, Mr and Mrs Isidor Straus, but not the Duff Gordons. Several *Titanic* passengers who had not been depicted before are included: the Countess of Rothes glimpsed sweeping through the dining room; American filmmaker Daniel Marvin and his wife Mary, newly married in England and whose marriage had actually been filmed; theatrical producer Henry B. Harris and his wife René; stewardess Violet Jessop whose memoirs were subsequently published under the title *Titanic Survivor*; Father Byles, the Catholic priest who comforted those on board the sinking ship; and notably Lawrence Beesley, the Dulwich College schoolmaster who wrote an account of the disaster, *The Loss of the Titanic*, published in 1913. Several of the vignettes of shipboard life recounted by Beesley are reproduced exactly. He was a genuine historical character but he is given an unfulfilled shipboard romance with an American schoolteacher, Leigh Goodwin, who is entirely fictitious. So much for authenticity.

In the interests of stripping away the myth, there is no 'Nearer, My God, to Thee'; they prefer the Anglican hymn 'Autumn'; there is no injunction to 'Be British'; no Guggenheim saying, 'We've dressed in our best and are prepared to go down like gentlemen'. But several characters claim that the ship is unsinkable. The causes of the disaster are duly given as the absence of lifeboat drills, shortage of lifeboats, ignored ice warnings, and full speed. At the end there is panic and firearms are used. The film includes the reality, previously glossed over, that John Jacob Astor (inexplicably bearded – Astor had a moustache only) was travelling with his pregnant eighteen-year-old second wife Madeleine whom he married after a controversial divorce from his first wife. He is snubbed on board by several acquaintances, but Molly Brown befriends Madeleine. Benjamin Guggenheim, having broken with his continental mistress, is returning home to the wife and family he had effectively abandoned. He and Astor meet and discuss whether the younger women really love them for themselves or for their money. But the millionaires behave well: Astor puts his wife in a boat and stays behind, the Strauses stay together, Molly Brown wants to return for survivors.

The class structure of the ship is made explicit when Leigh Goodwin says that the ship with its three classes is a 'microcosm of the British social system' and Beesley replies that it is the embodiment of the American economic system which allows the rich to buy the best of everything. The film gives equal weight to all three classes. The millionaires inhabit the first class; the two schoolteachers second; and the Irish emigrants the steerage. Although the historically authentic figures of Martin Gallagher, James Farrell and Daniel Buckley appear, the depiction of the steerage passengers is a highly sentimentalized, soft-focus view with the gorgeous colleens and feisty boyos drinking, singing, dancing and falling in love, only to be parted when the girls escape in lifeboats and the boys go down with the ship. In getting the girls to the lifeboats, the boys break down the locked iron gates, symbolically destroying the class barriers, and move awe-struck through the first-class dining room. All the scenes involving the steerage passengers seem to be directly modelled on those in *A Night to Remember*. The millionaires drown. The religious element is present with the intercutting of a Catholic service for the emigrants and a Protestant service conducted by the captain. As 'Eternal Father, strong to save ... for those in peril on the sea' is sung, the film cuts to approaching ice floes.

The moral to be drawn from the disaster is underlined in the final scene. Aboard the *Carpathia* Lawrence and Leigh say the disaster means the end of certainty and security: 'We'll never be able to look at the world in the same way.' A woman distributing coffee to the survivors says, 'It's God's will', and a stricken survivor replies, 'God went down with the *Titanic*'.

Despite the presence of eight stars (David Janssen, Cloris Leachman, Susan Saint James, David Warner, Harry Andrews, Helen Mirren,

Beverly Ross, Ian Holm) and a strong supporting cast of British character actors, the film was neither a box-office nor a critical success. Distinguished cinematographer Christopher Challis, hired to shoot the film, reflected ruefully on the experience in his autobiography.[3] He thought *A Night to Remember* 'excellent' and felt the eight-week shooting schedule for *S.O.S. Titanic* wholly inadequate, when compared to the five months *A Night to Remember* took to film. Extensive studio reconstruction was out of the question and so the first-class interiors were shot at the Waldorf Hotel in London and the Isle of Man ferry, *The Manxman*, was utilized for many of the exteriors, with the *Queen Mary*, now embedded in concrete at Long Beach, California, used for scenes on the bridge and long-shots. A section of the deck of *Titanic* and the steerage section were constructed in Shepperton studios and used for scenes of the sinking. The ludicrously small scale of *The Manxman* as a stand-in for the *Titanic*, the ragged continuity and loose ends created by the excision of half an hour from the television version and the deadening blandness characteristic of made-for-television films ensured that it failed to displace *A Night to Remember*.

Completely swamped by the world-wide wash from the 1997 block-buster, the television mini-series *Titanic* (1996), produced by the Konigsberg-Sanitsky Company in association with American Zoetrope and presented by Hallmark, was filmed in Canada, utilized up-to-date computer technology and was shown in the USA on the CBS network. In Britain, it was released on video. It returned full-scale to the *Grand Hotel* format but with equal time given to the first-class and steerage-class passengers. It starred Peter Gallagher, Eva Marie Saint, Catherine Zeta Jones and Tim Curry, all playing fictional characters, with Marilu Henner as Molly Brown and George C. Scott as Captain Smith.

The other historical figures included Bruce Ismay, the officers Murdoch, Lightoller, Boxhall and Lowe, Captain Rostron and Harold Cottam of *Carpathia*, Captain Lord of *Californian* and wireless officers Bride and Phillips, but omitted Thomas Andrews, the Duff Gordons and the Countess of Rothes. Among the passengers, the Astors, the Strauses and Benjamin Guggenheim appear, and for the first time Mr and Mrs Hudson Allison and their daughter Lorraine, the only first-class child to perish in the disaster. The causes of the disaster are given: shortage of lifeboats and binoculars, no red flares, delayed ice-warnings, and Murdoch ordering the ship to reverse rather than hitting the berg head on, which would not have damaged it fatally. The failure of *Californian* to respond is also featured. Most serious is Ismay ordering the ship to go at full speed to break the record for the Atlantic crossing, a charge of which Ismay had long been acquitted. But Ismay, portrayed by Roger Rees as neurotic and overbearing, is the obligatory British villain of contemporary Hollywood: determined to beat the record, overruling the captain and saving his own skin by escaping in a lifeboat.

The disaster serves as a background for two fictional love stories. In first class, Isabella Paradine, married to a man she does not love, renews an old love affair with Wynn Park; he drowns, she survives to be reunited with husband and child. In steerage Jamie Perse, cockney pickpocket who stole his ticket, falls for and is redeemed by Danish Christian emigrant Osa Ludwigssen.

There are luridly melodramatic subplots. Alice Cleaver, the neurotic cockney nursemaid of the Allisons, is haunted by premonitory dreams of a maritime disaster and awakes screaming from nightmares. She turns out to be an unmarried mother who killed her child but was released from prison on the grounds of her mental state. When disaster strikes she escapes with baby Trevor Allison, while the rest of the family stay on board looking for the child and go down with the ship. Irish steward Simon Doonan, a leering pantomime villain, blackmails Jamie into helping him rob the first-class staterooms, rapes Osa and escapes from the ship disguised as a woman. He is knocked out of the boat and drowns after he throws Osa into the sea when she recognizes him and accuses him.

The film intercuts between first class and steerage, with the steerage passengers singing and dancing, though not portrayed as Irish, and it includes Sunday service conducted by Captain Smith. Once the iceberg strikes, the events derive from Walter Lord's narrative and parallel *A Night to Remember*. Much of the action and dialogue at this stage is authentic. The Astors, who have been snubbed because of his re-marriage, are parted; Madeleine had befriended and advised the fictional Isabella. The Strauses stay behind with their famous dialogue. There is no Guggenheim in evening dress and no 'Nearer, My God, to Thee', but Captain Smith shouts 'Be British' at his crew and he quotes ironically a newspaper report headlined, 'God himself couldn't sink this ship'. More controversially, First Officer Murdoch shoots passengers and then shoots himself. The film even includes the apocryphal Astor comment: 'I asked for ice but this is ridiculous.' Steerage passengers are locked below decks. The scenes in the wireless room, aboard the *Carpathia* and on the lifeboats conform to the evidence. The Christian Jacks family who are left behind and pray together on deck, going down with the ship, recall the real-life Goodwin family who all perished. Snobbish and racist Hazel Foley who enters a lifeboat with her dog and her husband seems to be inspired by publisher Henry Sleeper Harper who got into a lifeboat with his wife, dog and Egyptian dragoman. The film ends with the arrival in New York: Molly Brown is a heroine, Alice Cleaver hands over baby Trevor to Allison's brother, Madeleine Astor is met by John's sons, Isabella is met by her husband and daughter.

Although 'Nearer, My God, to Thee', is dropped, redemption is a major theme of the film. Jamie is redeemed from his criminal life by love for Osa; Osa who loses her faith after being raped recovers it when both she and Jamie are saved; Alice Cleaver expiates the murder of her own child by saving baby Trevor from the wreck.

The characters are one-dimensional; plot-lines melodramatic; and some of the accents very uneasy; the actors with cockney accents seem to be graduates from the Dick Van Dyke Academy of Wonky Accents and the immigrants from Dorchester inexplicably speak with North Country accents.

The most spectacular version of the story of *Titanic* is the 1997 Fox production, written and directed by James Cameron. Running hugely over-budget and dogged by predictions of a disaster which would sink the studio, the film became upon release a phenomenal global success. It sold more tickets in its first year of release than any film in history, became the first film to gross one billion dollars world-wide and it garnered eleven Oscars at the Academy Awards.[4] To make the film, Fox had constructed a full-scale ship exterior at Rosarito in Baja California, Mexico, plus a fully equipped studio for the interior sets. It deployed all the wonders of modern computer technology and state of the art special effects wizardry to re-create the sinking.[5]

The film was part of a 1990s cycle of special effects spectaculars (*Independence Day, Armageddon, Deep Impact, Volcano, Twister, Jurassic Park*), all focusing on disasters, and all playing to deep-seated, almost atavistic, fears about the approaching millennium and what it might entail. But as Geoff King has argued, the spectacular scenes were deliberately designed to integrate the fictional romance.[6] It was actually a viewing of *A Night to Remember* in 1995 that inspired Cameron to make his own *Titanic*. He immediately dashed off a treatment and pitched it to the studio as 'Romeo and Juliet on the *Titanic*'. As he told an interviewer, he had been longing 'to do an epic romance in the traditional vein of *Gone with the Wind* and *Doctor Zhivago*'.[7] Cameron wrote in the introduction to the official account of the filming:

The tragedy has assumed an almost mythic quality in our collective imagination, but the passage of time has robbed it of its human face. Its status in our culture has become that of a morality tale, referred to more often as a metaphor in political cartoons than as an actual event. I set out to make a film that would bring the event to life, to humanize it, not a docudrama, but an experience in living history. I wanted to place the audience on the ship, in its final hours, to live out the tragic event in all its horribly fascinating glory. The greatest challenge of writing a new film about such an oft-told subject is the very fact that the story is so well known. What to say that hasn't been said? The only territory I felt had been left unexplored in prior films was the territory of the heart. I wanted the audience to cry for *Titanic*. Which means to cry for the *people* on the ship ... But the deaths of 1,500 innocents is too abstract for our hearts to grasp, although the mind can form the number easily. To fully experience the tragedy of *Titanic*, to be able to comprehend it in human terms, it seemed necessary to create an emotional lightning rod for the audience by giving them two main characters they care about and then taking these characters into hell. Jack and Rose were born out of this need, and the story of *TITANIC* became their story. I realized then that my film must be, first and always, a love story.[8]

In an interview, Cameron said: 'I thought it was not artistically interesting to just follow a bunch of historical characters, never really getting involved in the event at an emotional level.'[9] He thus distanced himself both from the docu-drama of *A Night to Remember* and the multi-strand format of following 'a bunch of historical characters' adopted by *S.O.S. Titanic*. Instead, he went for an ethos and approach much closer to those classic shipboard weepies, *One Way Passage* (1932) (doomed love affair on liner between two strangers, each with a secret: he is a convict being taken back to America to be executed; she has a fatal heart disease – but they will meet in the afterlife), *Now Voyager* (1942) (poor little rich girl liberated and glamorized by love for a wealthy married man after shipboard romance) and *An Affair to Remember* (1957) (shipboard romance between feckless aristocratic playboy and down-to-earth decent ordinary Boston Irish nightclub singer interrupted when she is crippled in an accident but ending in their reunion). There are echoes of all these stories in the story of Rose and Jack, in particular the basic theme that love conquers all barriers – death, injury or the marital status of one of the lovers.

Cameron's approach also explains why the genuine historical figures who appear in the film are marginalized, unless they have an ideological role to play. Thus John Jacob Astor, Benjamin Guggenheim, Sir Cosmo and Lady Duff Gordon, the Countess of Rothes, Colonel Archibald Gracie all appear but most of them only in a scene or two. The captain and officers, Ismay, Andrews and Molly Brown all have more substantial roles for reasons that will be explored later. But the focus on the love story, with such archetypal scenes as the lovers outlined on the prow against a blood-red sunset, Cal chasing the lovers round the sinking ship wildly firing a revolver, and Rose hacking at the handcuffs binding Jack to a pipe in the rapidly flooding brig, takes precedence over the historical episodes of the extraordinary seamanship of Captain Rostron and the desperate race of *Carpathia* to reach the scene of the disaster and the inexplicable inaction of the *Californian*. Scenes aboard the *Californian* were filmed but cut before release, confirming Cameron's decision to give the romantic narrative priority over the factual.

The audience appeal of the film, although it sought to merge romantic drama and action spectacle, was very markedly towards young women. Surveys revealed that 60 per cent of *Titanic*'s audience was female, 63 per cent of them under twenty-five and that 45 per cent of all women under twenty-five who went to see it had been at least twice, some of them many times.[10] One attraction was undoubtedly Leonardo di Caprio, who acquired a besotted following of pre-pubescent girls. For other young women, the leading figure, Rose De Witt Bukater (Kate Winslet), provided a contemporary identification figure for them, being characterized as a thoroughly modern miss, very much in the mould of previous strong-willed and independent-minded women at the centre of James Cameron films, notably *Aliens*, *Terminator 2* and *True Lies*. Rose collects Picasso paintings (which her fiancé despises), smokes in public (in defiance of her mother), and quotes Freud to Ismay (who asks if he is a passenger). But for her, the *Titanic* is not a 'ship of dreams' but 'a slave ship taking me back to America in chains'. She has been condemned to an arranged marriage with arrogant and patronizing steel heir Caledon Hockley because she and her mother have been left penniless after the death of her father. 'It's so unfair,' says Rose. 'Of course, it's unfair. We're women,' replies her mother, one of the film's many indictments of Edwardian class and gender attitudes. In her despair at the forced marriage, she plans to throw herself off the stern of the ship but is coaxed back on board by Jack Dawson (Leonardo di Caprio). The romance between first-class passenger Rose and steerage-class Jack is the central theme of the film; it is unlike the romance in *Titanic* (1953) which is between two first-class passengers, and the parallel romances in *Titanic* (1996) which are between passengers within first and steerage class respectively. This makes class a central theme of the film.

Rose is liberated by Jack, and her trip becomes a voyage towards freedom in the New World, in the classic myth of the emigrants' escape from the Old World, which is why, head covered in a shawl, she takes her place with the rescued steerage passengers on *Carpathia*, and why she looks up directly at the Statue of Liberty as she enters New York Harbor after her rescue.

Jack Dawson represents freedom and America. Orphaned at fifteen, he is a free spirit from Wisconsin, dresses like a Huck Finn or Tom Sawyer figure, smokes and gambles, and, in a symbolic proletarian moment, teaches Rose to spit. This contrasts with Giff Rogers teaching Annette Sawyer to dance the Navaho Rag – the symbol of a classless America. Jack has roamed the world as an artist, painted nude models in Paris, and he lives by his motto, 'Make it count', the equivalent of 'Carpe diem' (Seize the day), preached by another free spirit, English teacher Robin Williams in *Dead Poets Society*. He declares: 'I've got everything I need right here with me. I've got air in my lungs and a few blank sheets of paper. I mean, I love waking up in the morning not knowing what's going to happen, who I'm going to meet, where I'm going to wind up.' Jack stands for candour, spontaneity, honest emotion, acting on instinct, rejecting class, hierarchy, convention. Rose comes to share these values.

Yet throughout she also displays an independent spirit and frequently takes the lead in a reversal of traditional gender roles. She it is who insists on being sketched naked, who drags Jack into the back of the car in the *Titanic*'s hold and initiates their lovemaking, who slugs a steward who is dragging her away from Jack, who gives the finger to the pursuing Lovejoy and who rescues Jack from the flooding brig by severing his handcuffs with an axe. She leaves the lifeboat to rejoin him on the doomed ship and after her rescue defiantly gives her name as Rose Dawson. She tells the salvage men, 'He saved me in every way that a person can be saved', physically, spiritually and emotionally. He has saved her from a forced marriage and a pointless upper-class life, and set her on the path to an active, independent life – the photographs next to the bed of the elderly Rose show her riding horses, deep-sea fishing, flying airplanes and becoming a movie star. In the tradition of the grand Hollywood romances of Frank Borzage, it is primarily about the transforming power of love, a love that transcends death. The final sequence, either in Rose's death or her dreams (it is not made clear), she and Jack are reunited on the *Titanic*, applauded by the assembled passengers, no longer divided by class.

'We're holding just short of Marxist dogma,' joked Cameron.[11] But the indictment of the class system runs all through the film, most obviously in the cross-class love story, but also in the regular cross-cutting between first and steerage class from the start of the voyage where the first-class passengers arrive in a fleet of luxury cars and are ushered aboard without delay while the steerage passengers are lined up to be checked for lice. Then there is cutting between the stuffy and snobbish first-class dining room (with the gentlemen withdrawing to the smoking room for port and cigars, thus demonstrating their outdated male chauvinism) and steerage where the Irish emigrants (natural, decent, ordinary, warm) are having a 'hoolie' and where Rose kicks off her shoes and joins in, drinking beer, dancing wildly and rejoicing in liberation. Later, during the disaster, the third-class passengers are kept locked below decks while the first-class passengers are put into boats. Cameron says: 'The truth of the matter is that a third-class male on the *Titanic* stood a one-in-ten chance of surviving whereas a first-class female stood a nine-in-ten chance. I've explained those odds so the audience will understand exactly what kind of sacrifice Rose makes when she chooses to be with Jack.' In fact, while only 14 per cent of steerage-class males survived, only 10 per cent of second-class males survived, but the second class is omitted from Cameron's *Titanic*, in contrast to *S.O.S. Titanic*, thus rendering the class gulf more stark.

The symbol of the upper class is Caledon 'Cal' Hockley, the handsome, ruthless, arrogant steel magnate who is a domineering bully, with a slimy English manservant, Lovejoy, who spies on the lovers, frames Jack for theft and later leaves him handcuffed in the flooding brig. Cal uses a lost child in order to get into a lifeboat and survives but, as Rose relates, lost his fortune in the 1929 crash and shot himself. By contrast with Cal, the only one of the authentic first-class passengers to get extensive footage is Molly Brown, forthright, decent, down-to-earth, who befriends Jack and kits him out in her son's evening suit. She is a self-made mid-western ally.

Added to the attack on class there is a distinctly anti-English bias, not present in previous versions. The causes of the tragedy are duly identified as shortage of lifeboats, ignored ice warnings, not enough binoculars and excessive speed. But more significantly Bruce Ismay, the owner, orders the captain to go at full speed and later shamefacedly escapes in a lifeboat; Captain Smith is stunned by the tragedy and unable to act decisively; Lightoller (hero of *A Night to Remember*) is portrayed as a snooty upper-class figure sending off boats half-empty; two English stewards abandon Rose and Jack. Murdoch, the Scottish officer, takes a bribe from Hockley to secure a lifeboat place, shoots the lovable forthright Irishman Tommy Ryan and then shoots himself. Apart from Wallace Hartley and the band, the historical figures who act decently are the very obviously Welsh officer Lowe who goes back to look for survivors, and the Irish-accented Thomas Andrews, a genuinely tragic figure, sympathetic to Rose and Jack. The Irishman Tommy Ryan, who makes regular disparaging remarks about the first class and the English, leads the steerage break-out from below decks, slugging a steward who tries to stop them, and is finally shot by Murdoch. Cameron stressed that 'Accuracy is a big challenge for us. Wherever possible we want to tell our story within an absolutely rigorous, historically accurate framework, complementing history rather than distorting it.' Nevertheless, there are a number of departures from accuracy.[12] Lightoller, who took control of an upturned boat and navigated it to safety, was one of the heroes of the night and far from speaking with a *pukka* accent, had a rich West Country accent. In Scotland, there was outrage at the depiction of Murdoch, the story of whose suicide is vigorously contested, and who is regarded as a hero in his home town. Fox shamefacedly made an ex-gratia payment to the local school to assuage local feelings. Of the famous incidents of the disaster, a few are fleetingly re-created: Guggenheim appears and quotes the famous line, 'We've dressed up in our best and are prepared to go down like gentlemen'; *Titanic* buffs would recognize Mr and Mrs Straus huddled together on their bed, Father Byles leading passengers in prayer, Baker Charles Joughin taking a swig of brandy as he jumps into the water; but none of these characters is identified and most likely passed the general audience by. The Astors' parting is not included; the heroism and stoic chivalry of the upper classes is definitely not part of Cameron's agenda.

The film acknowledges one of the sources of the revived interest in the *Titanic* story – the discovery of the wreck. The film's narrative is recounted in a framing story which becomes an anti-materialist fable. A group of greedy, profane, cynical and uncouth treasure-hunters is exploring the wreck in search of the fabulous jewel 'Heart of the Ocean', believed to be in the safe in Hockley's stateroom. It is not there but 101-year-old Mrs Rose Calvert contacts them and tells them the story, not revealing that she has the jewel which, after telling her story, she throws into the sea to join the wreck. At the end, Brock Lovett, the chief treasure-hunter, tells Rose's granddaughter that he'd been living with the *Titanic* for three years – 'But I never got it – I never let it in.' In other words, he has until now not appreciated the human dimensions of the tragedy. The wreck was simply a chance for plunder. Rose's story has in a way liberated him.

With its emphasis on female liberation, freedom of choice, the primacy of spontaneity, instincts and 'let it all hang out' emotion, hostility to materialism, class privilege and the English, this is very much a film in tune with the sensibilities of 1990s Hollywood and beyond that of liberal Clintonian America.

CONCLUSION

The power of the *Titanic* to stir audiences is confirmed by the regularity with which the cinema has returned to it as a subject for drama. It is a classical tragedy of epic proportions, moving from *hubris* to *nemesis* and containing in almost equal measure pathos, irony and allegory. Of the seven major screen versions since the coming of sound (1929, 1943, 1953, 1958, 1979, 1996, 1997), the best, according to informed opinion, is *A Night to Remember*. Almost all the others have used the historical events and characters as background to fictional romantic melodramas. But *A Night to Remember* is a docu-drama on an epic scale, a film which stirs the emotions while you are watching it and haunts the memory thereafter. It is not the absolute truth because it uses composite characters, concentrates on the British experience of the tragedy and incorporates errors which have been identified by subsequent research, but it is as close to the truth as any film is likely to get. Like all films, it is a product of its times but in its innate integrity, documentary authenticity, emotional truthfulness and celebration of heroic stoicism it transcends its own period to become timeless and universal. It is because audiences now as much as when it was released can identify with the predicaments of a shipload of men and women of all backgrounds, ages and classes who are suddenly and violently confronted with the prospect of death. There but for the grace of God go all of us.

Since its rapturous reception at its British première, the film has been shown all round the world. It has had regular television showings in Britain (1979, 1988, 1991, 1993, 1996, 1998). It has been released on video and on DVD. It has been the subject of a documentary about its making. The discovery of the wreck in 1985 and the ballyhoo surrounding James

Cameron's 1997 *Titanic* only served to increase the interest in *A Night to Remember*. It is a tribute to the vision, commitment and loving care which William MacQuitty, Roy Baker, Eric Ambler and their production team devoted to the project that more than forty years after its first release, *A Night to Remember* remains the definitive *Titanic* film, a film not only to remember but to cherish.

APPENDIX
▬▬ Nearer, My God, to Thee ▬▬

Cinema may have a role to play in solving one of the continuing debates about the *Titanic*. One of the most enduring legends associated with the *Titanic* is the identity of the last piece of music to be played as the ship went down. It is a matter of undisputed fact that the *Titanic*'s eight musicians, led by bandmaster Wallace Hartley, stood on deck playing ragtime tunes, waltzes and other pieces of light music from their repertoire to keep the passengers calm as the lifeboats were filled. But after this, as the ship began to tilt and the end approached, Hartley told his musicians that they had done their duty and should look to themselves. Before they dispersed they played one final tune. None of them survived the wreck, but the memory of their calmness and courage immortalized them. Typical of the popular view of them was that of survivor Lawrence Beesley who wrote in his book *The Loss of the S.S. Titanic*: 'Many brave things were done that night but none more brave than by those few men playing minute after minute as the ship settled quietly lower and lower in the sea and the sea rose higher and higher where they stood – the music they played serving alike as their own immortal requiem and their right to be recorded on the rolls of undying fame.'[1]

Word spread rapidly after the news of the disaster broke that the last tune they had played was the hymn 'Nearer, My God, to Thee'. This symbol of Christian resignation and acceptance of the will of God reinforced the image of stoicism and humility that the public wanted to hear in accounts of the story. Newspapers highlighted the story, sheet music of the hymn was produced, adorned by portraits of the musicians, picture postcards were issued containing the words of the hymn, all of them attesting to the continuing strength of the Christian faith after a century of doubt.

The British Musicians' Union sold copies of the hymn, bearing the portraits of the bandsmen, to raise money for their families. On 24 May 1912, Empire Day, the seven chief London orchestras put on a concert at the Royal Albert Hall in memory of the musicians who had perished. Five hundred musicians performed, conducted in turn by Sir Edward Elgar, Sir Henry Wood, Landon Ronald, Thomas Beecham, Percy Pitt and Willem Mengelberg, who had travelled specially from Berlin to take part. Madame Ada Crossley sang 'O, Rest in the Lord' from Mendelssohn's *Elijah*. The programme included Chopin's *Funeral March*, Elgar's *Enigma Variations*, Sullivan's overture *In Memoriam* and the third movement of Tchaikovsky's *Pathetique* symphony. The *Daily Sketch* (25 May 1912) reported:

> The supreme moment of the day came when Sir Henry Wood led the orchestra through the first eight bars of Dykes' version of 'Nearer, My God, to Thee' and then, turning to the audience, he conducted the singing to the end – quite 10,000 people, intense with emotion, sang in unison what is now one of the world's most famous hymns, and the effect was such that women wept and men had difficulty in mastering their feelings ... To two ladies sitting in a box near the Royal party, the hymn made special appeal, and their emotions were evident. The last time they had heard it was from a small boat laden to the water's edge and the band playing the hymn on the boat deck of the sinking *Titanic*.

In recent years, however, there has been a sustained assault on the myth. Walter Lord, that indefatigable seeker of *Titanic* memories, declared in his book *A Night to Remember* that he believed the final music to have been played was the Anglican hymn 'Autumn'.[2] This was based entirely on the memories of one man, wireless officer Harold Bride, who in an interview with the *New York Times* (19 April 1912) recalled that the last piece he heard the band play as he swam away from the ship was 'Autumn'. This story gained increasing credence after Walter Lord endorsed it in *A Night to Remember*. However, 'Autumn' presents even more problems than 'Nearer, My God, to Thee'. As the historian of hymns Ian Bradley wrote:

> There are, in fact, three different tunes with this name to be found in early twentieth-century hymn-books, set respectively to Robert Bridges's 'Joy and triumph everlasting', George Horne's 'See the leaves around us falling', and William Walsham How's 'The year is swiftly waning'. If it was one of these that the band played, the last is the most likely candidate. The lines which close its first verse would certainly have been appropriate to the melancholy occasion:

> And life, brief life, is speeding:
> The end is nearing fast.[3]

In fact, the whole 'Autumn' story is a dangerous red herring. Bride never calls 'Autumn' a hymn and he does not say it was the last piece to be played, only that it was the last piece he heard. It was other newspapers reproducing the highlights of the original interview that identified 'Autumn' as a hymn, presumably on the assumption that the final piece to be played had to be a hymn.

As a matter of fact, people never refer to hymns by the names of their tunes but by their first lines, and Archibald Joyce's popular waltz 'Songe d'Automne' (informally called 'Autumn') is known to have been one of the pieces in the repertoire of the *Titanic*'s band. It is quite likely that it was played to soothe the passengers. But this does not invalidate the playing of 'Nearer, My God, to Thee' as the final gesture. When Walter Lord reviewed the evidence in *The Night Lives On* (1986), he confirmed that Bride had never called 'Autumn' a hymn and was alluding to Joyce's waltz, but he continued to insist on it as the last piece to be played.[4] This view still depends exclusively on the Bride interview. No one else mentioned 'Autumn'.

There remains, however, a good deal of evidence in favour of 'Nearer, My God, to Thee'. Richard Howells, claiming that the story spread upon the arrival of the survivors in New York, suggests that the true story that passengers sang 'Nearer, My God, to Thee' when the steamship *Valencia* sank in 1906 was transferred to the *Titanic* because it was appropriate.[5] But the *Valencia* story – and it is only one of several maritime disaster accounts that that involve passengers singing hymns on stricken ships – makes it more likely rather than less that 'Nearer, My God, to Thee' *was* played on *Titanic*. Herman Finck, musical director of the Theatre Royal, Drury Lane, recalled the testimony of his principal violinist, George Orrell, who had been bandmaster on the *Carpathia*, the liner which raced to the aid of the *Titanic* and picked up the survivors. This indicates that the story pre-dated the arrival in New York. Finck writes:

> From the survivors, he received the story of how the *Titanic*'s band, with wonderful courage, played 'Nearer, My God, to Thee' as the ship sank. 'The ship's band in any emergency,' he relates, 'is expected to play to calm the passengers.' After the *Titanic* struck the iceberg the band began to play bright music, dance music, comic songs – anything that would prevent the passengers from becoming panic-stricken. The ship

was so badly holed that it was soon obvious that disaster was ahead. Then various awe-stricken passengers began to think of the death that faced them and asked the bandmaster to play hymns. The one which appealed to all was 'Nearer, My God, to Thee'. And soon the liner broke in two and sank, with fourteen hundred people on board; among them the eight gallant musicians.[6]

Charlotte Collyer, a grocer's wife from Hampshire who was travelling with her husband and daughter to a new life in Idaho, survived with her daughter but lost her husband. She wrote to her parents-in-law on 21 April, breaking the news and adding, 'When that band played "Nearer, my God, to Thee" I know he thought of you and me for we both loved that hymn.'[7] Others who recalled hearing it were stewardess Violet Jessop, Chief Steward Edward Wheelton, and first-class passenger Mrs Vera Dick.[8]

To set against this, American survivor Colonel Archibald Gracie emphatically testified that it had not been played. He recalled that the band played: 'I did not recognize any of the tunes, but I know they were cheerful and were not hymns. If, as has been reported, "Nearer, My God, to Thee" was one of the selections, I assuredly should have noticed it and regarded it as a tactless warning of immediate death to us all.'[9] He reported that none of the people he had questioned recalled it being played, but there may be a very good reason for this.

Mrs Sarah Flower Adams's hymn was published in 1841. Several tunes were fitted to it. But it became particularly associated with two tunes, both of them memorable, stirring and uplifting, 'Horbury' (1861) by the British minister Reverend John Bacchus Dykes, and 'Bethany' (1856) by the American Dr Lowell Mason. 'Horbury' was most often used when the hymn was sung in Britain and 'Bethany' when it was sung in America. This may explain the diametrically opposed memories of the survivors. If as is likely the band were playing the British version of the hymn, the American survivors would not necessarily have recognized it.

There is a further complication. There was a third tune attached to the hymn, Sir Arthur Sullivan's 'Propior Deo'. Unlike 'Horbury', which was the preferred Anglican version, 'Propior Deo' was the tune most favoured by the Nonconformists and never appeared in the great Anglican hymnal *Hymns Ancient and Modern*. This is significant because Wallace Hartley was a devout Methodist, son of a long-serving Methodist choirmaster and is known to have favoured this version of the hymn. His family were so firmly convinced that this would have been the version chosen by him that they had the opening bars of 'Propior Deo' carved on the monument above his grave at Colne. Hartley's body was recovered from the sea, his violin strapped to his chest, and returned to Britain. Thirty thousand mourners attended his funeral in Colne and the Bethel Choir and the Colne Orchestral Society sang 'Nearer, My God, to Thee'. Sadly, Sullivan's version is rather humdrum and undistinguished and lacks the sense of uplift to be found in both the Dykes and Mason versions. Both the Dykes and Sullivan versions of the hymn appeared in the British *Titanic* memorabilia. Interestingly, when the Danish composer Carl Nielsen composed his *Paraphrase on* 'Nearer, My God, to Thee' in the aftermath of the tragedy in 1912, he opted for the Lowell Mason tune. 'Horbury' was used at the Royal Albert Hall memorial concert. Whatever the tune actually played, the case for 'Nearer, My God, to Thee' remains very strong. It is enhanced by the testimony of Mr E. Moody, who played with Hartley in the orchestra aboard the *Mauretania* and asked him what he would do if he were on a sinking liner. Hartley replied that he would get his men together and play either 'O God, Our Help in Ages Past' or 'Nearer, My God, to Thee'. 'They are both favourite hymns of mine and they would be very suitable for the occasion,' said Hartley.[10] 'Nearer, My God, to Thee' was also traditionally played at the funeral of a member of the Musicians' Union.

As a footnote to the heroism of the musicians, it might be noted that the White Star Line refused the musicians' families compensation on the grounds that they were not employees of the company, only second-class passengers, because the musicians had been supplied to the ship by an agency, C. W. and F. N. Black of Liverpool. Black's reaction to the tragedy was to send a bill to the father of one of the drowned musicians, Jock Hume, for the cost of his uniform. In the end the Titanic Relief Fund decided to include the musicians among the crew for the purposes of charitable relief and the families were able to draw on their extensive funds.

It is here that the cinematic evidence has something to offer. Of those film versions which have played 'Nearer, My God, to Thee', the American versions of *Titanic* (1953, 1997) have used the American Lowell Mason tune, as did the American film of *Cavalcade* (1932) in its *Titanic* sequence, and *History is Made at Night* (1937) in its *Titanic* pastiche. But the British film *A Night to Remember* (1958) uses the British tune 'Horbury' by Dykes. Despite the fact that the film was based on Lord's book and Lord had plumped for the Anglican hymn tune

'Autumn', producer William MacQuitty went for 'Nearer, My God, to Thee'. He had consulted fifty of the survivors and was persuaded by their firm conviction that the hymn had been played. Survivors Edith Russell and Eva Hart, who both became friends of MacQuitty, were in particular adamant that it was 'Nearer, My God, to Thee'.[11] This tends to confirm the divergence between Britain and America in the matter of the appropriate tune. What is more curious is that the Nazi version of *Titanic* also opted for Lowell Mason's tune. This may be because it was the tune used in the trilingual (English–French–German) film *Atlantic* in 1929, which would have been familiar to the German filmmakers as it was the first ever German talkie. Reflecting the new orthodoxy inspired by Walter Lord, the 1956 live NBC-TV version of *A Night to Remember* featured the Anglican hymn tune 'Autumn'; so too did *S.O.S. Titanic*. The 1996 television mini-series *Titanic* opted for Archibald Joyce's 'Autumn' as the final music, but it is lost amid the general panic. There is no doubt that sequences in which the orchestra on the doomed ship plays 'Nearer, My God, to Thee' (whether in the Mason or Dykes versions) have a powerful mythic and spiritual resonance which is wholly absent from the versions in which 'Autumn' is played. It may however turn out to be the case that the version of 'Nearer, My God, to Thee' actually played was Sullivan's, which no film has ever deployed.

Notes

1. THE BACKGROUND

1. The precise numbers of passengers and survivors are still disputed, the difficulty being, as Richard Howells explains, 'the stowaways, deserters, passengers joining and leaving in France and Ireland, and inaccuracies in the passenger list'. I have followed the figures given by Howells, *Myth of the Titanic*, pp. 18, 165.

2. Ibid., p. 34; Cox, *The Titanic Story*, p. 33.

3. The best accounts and analyses of the *Titanic* myth are Howells, *Myth of the Titanic*, and Biel, *Down with the Old Canoe*.

4. Girouard, *Return to Camelot*; Fraser, *America and the Patterns of Chivalry*.

5. Howells, *Myth of the Titanic*, p. 82.

6. Richards, *Films and British National Identity*, p. 20.

7. Howells, *Myth of the Titanic*, pp. 82–3; Biel, *Down with the Old Canoe*, p. 25.

8. Howells, *Myth of the Titanic*, p. 101.

9. Davie, *The Titanic*, p. 68.

10. Gracie, *Titanic*, p. 34.

11. Biel, *Down with the Old Canoe*, p. 48.

12. Ibid., p. 38.

13. Ibid., p. 46.

14. Davie, *The Titanic*, p. 63.

15. Mersey Inquiry Report, *The Loss of the Titanic, 1912*, pp. 106–7.

16. Ibid., p. 178.

17. Howells, *Myth of the Titanic*, p. 96.

18. Lord, *A Night to Remember*, p. 73.

19. *Daily Sketch*, 22 April 1912.

20. Lord, *A Night to Remember*, pp. 10, 138.

21. There is a complete account of the Titanic and the silent cinema in Bottomore, *The Titanic and Silent Cinema*. See also Mills, *The Titanic in Pictures*, pp. 17–21.

22. Barrow, *On Q*, p. 57.

23. Raymond, *Please You, Draw Near* (London, p. 24).

24. Mills, *The Titanic in Pictures*, p. 24.

25. Mills, *The Titanic in Pictures*, pp. 26–31.

26. *The Times*, 18 November 1929.

27. Raymond, *Please You, Draw Near*, p. 26.
28. Moseley, *Evergreen*, p. 51.
29. The English characters of *Atlantic* were converted directly into Germans. John Rool became Heinrich Thomas, Second Officer Lanchester became Second Officer Lersner and Harry, Clara and Betty Tate-Hughes became Harry, Clara and Betty von Schröder. The only real differences from the English-language version were that the Latin 'Dandy' became the German Poldi, was markedly more hysterical than 'Dandy', and being played by popular musical star Willi Forst was given a song to perform at the piano, and Major Boldy became Doctor Holtz and led the prayers at the end.
30. Thomas, *Selznick*, pp. 187–8; Taylor, *Hitch*, pp. 148–9; Schaefer, 'The sinking of David O. Selznick's "Titanic"', pp. 57–73; Mills, *The Titanic in Pictures*, pp. 34–40.
31. Strobl, *The Germanic Isle*.
32. Hull, *Film in the Third Reich*, p. 231.
33. Ibid., pp. 226–9.
34. The story of the post-war history of *Titanic* is told by Robert Peck, 'The Banning of *Titanic*', pp. 427–44.
35. Higham and Greenberg, *The Celluloid Muse*, p. 195.
36. Ibid.
37. Hull, *Film in the Third Reich*, p. 226.
38. Solomon, *Twentieth Century-Fox*, p. 248.
39. Di Orio, *Barbara Stanwyck*, p. 156.
40. Ibid., p. 155.
41. Solomon, *Twentieth Century-Fox*, p. 255.
42. Biel, *Down with the Old Canoe*, p. 83.

2. THE MAKING OF THE FILM

1. MacQuitty, *A Life to Remember*, pp. 5, 6, 322.
2. Mills, *The Titanic in Pictures*, p. 67.
3. William MacQuitty, interview in *The Making of A Night to Remember*, documentary film (Ray Johnson productions, 1993).
4. Porter, 'Methodism versus the Market-Place', pp. 129–30.
5. MacQuitty, *Titanic Memories*, p. 9; Baker, *The Director's Cut*, p. 104.
6. *Sunday Dispatch*, 6 July 1958.
7. *Daily Herald*, 4 July 1957.
8. Author's interview with William MacQuitty, 31 May 2001.
9. Author's interview with Roy Ward Baker, 25 April 2001.
10. McFarlane, *An Autobiography of British Cinema*, p. 49.
11. MacQuitty, *Titanic Memories*, p. 11.
12. Baker, *The Director's Cut*, p. 12.

13. MacQuitty, *A Life to Remember*, p. 323.
14. Baker, *The Director's Cut*, p. 62.
15. Ibid., pp. 101–3; MacQuitty, *Titanic Memories*, p. 25.
16. Baker, *The Director's Cut*, p. 102.
17. Author's interview with Roy Ward Baker.
18. MacQuitty, *A Life to Remember*, p. 234; Baker, *The Director's Cut*, p. 100.
19. Baker, *The Director's Cut*, p. 100.
20. Ibid., p. 101.
21. More, *More or Less*, p. 202.
22. MacQuitty, *Titanic Memories*, p. 12.
23. Baker, *The Director's Cut*, p. 101.
24. Walter Lord, interview in *The Making of A Night to Remember*.
25. MacQuitty, *Titanic Memories*, pp. 22, 24.
26. Jessop, *Titanic Survivor*, p. 233.
27. MacQuitty, *Titanic Memories*, p. 11.
28. McFarlane, *Autobiography of British Cinema*, p. 51.
29. Author's interview with Roy Ward Baker.
30. Maxford, 'Call Sheet', p. 77.
31. Author's interview with Roy Ward Baker.
32. Baker, *The Director's Cut*, p. 95.
33. More, *More or Less*, p. 202.
34. Shipman, *The Great Stars: the International Years*, p. 373.
35. *Daily Mail*, 28 October 1957.
36. Author's interviews with William MacQuitty and Roy Ward Baker.
37. McFarlane, *Autobiography of British Cinema*, p. 64.
38. *The Star*, 30 September 1957.
39. More, *More or Less*, p. 203; MacQuitty, *A Life to Remember*, p. 326.
40. Maxford, 'Call Sheet', p. 78.
41. Mills, *The Titanic in Pictures*, p. 41.
42. *Manchester Guardian*, 1 November 1957.
43. MacQuitty, *Titanic Memories*, p. 14; Baker, *The Director's Cut*, p. 102.
44. More, *More or Less*, p. 204.
45. Maxford, 'Call Sheet', p. 79.
46. Baker, *The Director's Cut*, pp. 37–8.
47. Murphy, *The British Cinema and the Second World War*, p. 124.
48. Author's interview with William MacQuitty.
49. Baker, *The Director's Cut*, p. 95.
50. Ibid., p. 22.
51. McFarlane, *Autobiography of British Cinema*, p. 550.
52. Durgnat, *A Mirror for England*, pp. 206, 239–40, 166.

53. Ambler, *Here Lies Eric Ambler*, p. 226.
54. Durgnat, *A Mirror for England*, p. 242.
55. *Daily Mail*, 22 February 1950; *The Star*, 21 February 1950.
56. Mills, *Up in the Clouds, Gentlemen Please*, p. 213.
57. Hutchings, 'Authorship and British Cinema: the Case of Roy Ward Baker', p. 181.
58. Author's interview with Roy Ward Baker.
59. McFarlane, *Autobiography of British Cinema*, p. 49.
60. Author's interview with Roy Ward Baker.
61. Baker, *The Director's Cut*, pp. 106, 111.
62. Ibid., p. 113; McFarlane, *Autobiography of British Cinema*, pp. 416, 70.
63. *Monthly Film Bulletin*, 28 (February 1961), p. 20.
64. McFarlane, *Autobiography of British Cinema*, p. 51.
65. Baker, *The Director's Cut*, p. 125.
66. Pitt, *Life's a Scream*, p. 208.
67. Brosnan, *The Horror People*, p. 224.
68. Hutchings, 'Authorship and British Cinema', pp. 179–89.
69. Ambler, *Here Lies Eric Ambler*, p. 226.
70. Lambert, *The Dangerous Edge*, p. 131.
71. Wilcox, *Twenty-Five Thousand Sunsets*, pp. 196–200.
72. Ibid., p. 197.
73. Ambler, 'The Novelist and the Film-makers', pp. 217–18.
74. Walter Lord, interview in *The Making of A Night to Remember*.

3. A CRITICAL ANALYSIS OF THE FILM

1. Baker, 'Discovering Where the Truth Lies', pp. 17, 38.
2. Baker, *The Director's Cut*, pp. 48–9.
3. Aitken (ed.), *The Documentary Movement*, pp. 205, 213–14.
4. Author's interviews with Roy Ward Baker and William MacQuitty.
5. Lubin, *Titanic*, pp. 77–8.
6. Powell, *Films Since 1939*, pp. 22, 29, 40.
7. Manvell, *Twenty Years of British Film 1925–1945*, pp. 84–5.
8. See the discussion in detail in Richards, *Films and British National Identity*, pp. 85–127.
9. Author's interview with Roy Ward Baker.

4. POST-PRODUCTION

1. *Daily Telegraph*, 4 July 1958.
2. Reported in *The Times*, 29 May 1953.

3. Ellis, 'Art, Culture, Quality', pp. 9–49.
4. Elley (ed.), *Variety Movie Guide*, p. 424.
5. MacQuitty, interview in *The Making of A Night to Remember*.
6. More, *More or Less*, pp. 213, 214.
7. Author's interviews with Roy Ward Baker and William MacQuitty.
8. Bogdanor and Skidelsky (eds), *The Age of Affluence*, p. 7.
9. Durgnat, *A Mirror for England*, pp. 149–50.
10. Dixon, 'Roy Ward Baker', p. 28.
11. Howells, 'Atlantic Crossings: Nation, Class and Identity in *Titanic* (1953) and *A Night to Remember* (1958)', pp. 421–38.
12. Lubin, *Titanic*, pp. 76, 73.

5. THE *TITANIC* AND THE CINEMA: AFTER *A NIGHT TO REMEMBER*

1. Higham and Greenberg, *The Celluloid Muse*, p. 195; MacQuitty, *A Life to Remember*, p. 323.
2. Mills, *The Titanic in Pictures*, p. 84.
3. Challis, *Are They Really So Awful?*, pp. 213–17.
4. Lubin, *Titanic*, p. 7.
5. For the official account of the filming, see Marsh, *James Cameron's Titanic*. For an unofficial and rather more caustic account, see Jarvis, *Acting Strangely*, pp. 197–208. Jarvis, who plays Sir Cosmo Duff Gordon in Cameron's film, describes *A Night to Remember* as 'the best and most authentic account of the disaster' (p. 199).
6. King, *Spectacular Narratives*, p. 58.
7. Krämer, 'Women First: *Titanic* (1997), Action Adventure Films and Hollywood's Female Audience', p. 614. *Guardian*, 2 January 1998, on the origins of the film.
8. Marsh, *James Cameron's Titanic*, pp. v–vi.
9. Krämer, 'Women First', p. 606.
10. Lubin, *Titanic*, p. 10.
11. Marsh, *James Cameron's Titanic*, p. 73.
12. Ibid., p. 126.

APPENDIX

1. Beesley, *The Loss of the S.S. Titanic*, pp. 54–5.
2. Lord, *A Night to Remember*, p. 201.
3. Bradley, *The Penguin Book of Hymns*, p. 283.
4. Lord, *The Night Lives On*, pp. 119–48.
5. Howells, *The Myth of the Titanic*, pp. 129–30.

6. Finck, *My Melodious Memories*, pp. 109–10.

7. Foster (ed.), *Titanic*, p. 90.

8. Jessop, *Titanic Survivor*, p.132; *New York Times*, 19 April 1912 (Mrs Vera Dick); *Daily Sketch*, 20 April 1912 (Edward Wheelton).

9. Gracie, *Titanic*, p. 20.

10. *Daily Sketch*, 22 April 1912.

11. Author's interview with William MacQuitty.

Sources

INTERVIEWS

Author's interview with Roy Ward Baker, 25 April 2001.

Author's interview with William MacQuitty, 31 May 2001.

Interviews with William MacQuitty and Walter Lord in the film *The Making of A Night to Remember* (Ray Johnson Productions, 1993).

BOOKS AND ARTICLES

Aitken, Ian (ed.), *The Documentary Movement: An Anthology* (Edinburgh, 1998).

Ambler, Eric, 'The Novelist and the Film-Makers', in *The Ability to Kill and Other Pieces* (London, 1963), pp. 209–22.

—— *Here Lies Eric Ambler* (London, 1985).

Baker, Roy Ward, 'Discovering Where the Truth Lies', *Films and Filming* 7, (1961), pp. 17, 38.

—— *The Director's Cut* (London, 2000).

Barrow, Kenneth, *On Q* (Richmond, 1992).

Beesley, Lawrence, *The Loss of the S.S. Titanic* [1912] (Boston, 2000).

Biel, Steven, *Down with the Old Canoe: A Cultural History of the Titanic Disaster* (New York, 1996).

Bottomore, Stephen, *The Titanic and Silent Cinema* (Hastings, 2000).

Bradley, Ian, *The Penguin Book of Hymns* (London, 1991).

Brosnan, John, *The Horror People* (London, 1976).

Challis, Christopher, *Are They Really So Awful?* (London, 1993).

Cox, Stephen, *The Titanic Story* (Chicago and La Salle, IL, 1999).

Davie, Michael, *The Titanic* (London, 1986).

Di Orio, Al, *Barbara Stanwyck* (London, 1983).

Dixon, Wheeler Winston, 'Roy Ward Baker', *Classic Images*, 235 (January 1995), pp. 22–30.

Durgnat, Raymond, *A Mirror for England* (London, 1970).

Eaton, John P. and Charles A. Haas, *Titanic: Destination Disaster* (Yeovil, 1996).

Elley, Derek (ed.), *Variety Movie Guide* (London, 1991).

Ellis, John, 'Art, Culture, Quality', *Screen*, 19 (Autumn 1978), pp. 9–49.

Finck, Herman, *My Melodious Memories* (London, 1937).

Foster, John Wilson, *The Titanic Complex* (Vancouver, 1997).

— (ed.), *Titanic* (London, 1997).

Fraser, John, *America and the Patterns of Chivalry* (Cambridge, 1982).

Girouard, Mark, *Return to Camelot: Chivalry and the English Gentleman* (New Haven, CT, and London, 1981).

Gracie, Colonel Archibald, *Titanic* [1913] (Stroud, 1994).

Higham, Charles and Joel Greenberg, *The Celluloid Muse* (London, 1969).

Hirschhorn, Andrew, 'A Drama-documentary to Remember?', *Film Reader*, 2 (2000), pp. 38–42.

Howells, Richard, *The Myth of the Titanic* (Basingstoke and London, 1999).

— 'Atlantic Crossings: Nation, Class and Identity in *Titanic* (1953) and *A Night to Remember* (1958)', *Historical Journal of Film, Radio and Television*, 19 (October 1999), pp. 421–38.

Hull, David Stewart, *Film in the Third Reich* (Berkeley and Los Angeles, 1969).

Hutchings, Peter, 'Authorship and British Cinema: the Case of Roy Ward Baker', in Justine Ashby and Andrew Higson (eds), *British Cinema Past and Present* (London, 2000), pp. 179–89.

Jarvis, Martin, *Acting Strangely* (London, 1999).

Jessop, Violet, *Titanic Survivor* (ed. John Maxtone-Graham) (Stroud, 1998).

King, Geoff, *Spectacular Narratives* (London, 2000).

Krämer, Peter, 'Women First: *Titanic* (1997), Action Adventure Films and Hollywood's Female Audience', *Historical Journal of Film, Radio and Television*, 18 (October 1998), pp. 599–618.

Lambert, Gavin, *The Dangerous Edge* (New York, 1976).

Lightoller, C. H., *Titanic and Other Ships* (London, 1935).

Lord, Walter, *A Night to Remember* [1956] (London, 1987).

— *The Night Lives On* (London, 1986).

Lubin, David M., *Titanic* (London, 1999).

McFarlane, Brian, *An Autobiography of British Cinema* (London, 1997).

MacQuitty, William, *A Life to Remember* (London, 1991).

— *Titanic Memories* (Greenwich, 2000).

Manvell, Roger, *Twenty Years of British Films 1925–1945* (London, 1947).

Marsh, Ed, *James Cameron's Titanic* (London, 1998).

Maxford, Howard, 'Call Sheet: A Night to Remember', *Film Review*, 592 (April 2000), pp. 74–9.

Mersey Inquiry Report, *The Loss of the Titanic, 1912* (London, 1999).

Mills, John, *Up in the Clouds, Gentlemen Please* (London, 1980).

Mills, Simon, *The Titanic in Pictures* (Chesham, 1995).

More, Kenneth, *More or Less* (London, 1979).

Moseley, Roy, *Evergreen: Victor Saville in His Own Words* (Carbondale, IL, 2000).

Murphy, Robert, *The British Cinema and the Second World War* (London, 2000).

Peck, Robert, 'The Banning of *Titanic*: a Study in British Post-war Censorship in Germany', *Historical Journal of Film, Radio and Television*, 20 (August 2000), pp. 427–44.

Pitt, Ingrid, *Life's a Scream* (London, 1999).

Porter, Vincent, 'Methodism versus the Market-Place: the Rank Organization and British Cinema', in Robert Murphy (ed.), *The British Cinema Book* (London, 1997), pp. 122–32.

Powell, Dilys, *Films Since 1939* (London, 1947).

Raymond, Ernest, *Please You, Draw Near* (London, 1969).

Richards, Jeffrey, *Films and British National Identity* (Manchester, 1997).

Schaefer, Eric, 'The Sinking of David O. Selznick's "Titanic"', *Library Chronicle of the University of Texas at Austin*, 36 (1986), pp. 57–73.

Shipman, David, *The Great Stars: the International Years* (London, 1972).

Solomon, Aubrey, *Twentieth Century-Fox: A Corporate and Financial History* (Lanham, MD 1988).

Strobl, Gerwin, *The Germanic Isle* (Cambridge, 2000).

Taylor, John Russell, *Hitch* (New York, 1978).

Thomas, Bob, *Selznick* (New York, 1972).

Wilcox, Herbert, *Twenty-Five Thousand Sunsets* (London, 1967).